LIFE
LOVE
& LOCKUP

My Pain Became My Character

LIFE
LOVE
& LOCKUP
My Pain Became My Character

MICHELLE S. LOVETT, CURATOR

Atlanta, GA

DEDICATION

I dedicate this volume to my parents, Bennie & Gloria (RIP) Lovett; all my siblings; nieces; nephews; single parents; and men and women who tackle life without parents, family, friends; all those who fell victim to the streets; those that are battling illnesses and addictions; lupus warriors; domestic violence survivors; and individuals who are currently incarcerated or have been before. I salute all fighters who took a loss, regrouped, fought again and never lost faith. I've been through everything including death. However, my pain became my character.

CONTENTS

ACKNOWLEDGEMENTS

I would like to thank God, who is the head of my life, for giving me a second chance at life. God did it all. My father and best friend Bennie Lovett who decided to share his personal testimony in this volume (breaking his silence). Dad, thanks for your continuous love, loyalty, guidance and support. C. Nathaniel Brown, thank you for your continued daily coaching, mentorship and instructions. I certainly thank you for forwarding and blessing Volume 2 with your expertise. I'm thankful God teamed up two praying angels. Let us continue to receive instructions from our heavenly Father to bless others by providing a gateway for them to share their stories. I extend my appreciation and thanks to my team for believing in this project, Life, Love & Lockup, (9 KINGS & A QUEEN)! Thank you for collaborating and sharing your stories, reliving situations, praying, uncovering hurt and escaping custody. Your dedication, motivation, empowerment, advice, encouragement, expertise and overall efforts made this all possible.

FOREWORD

From the time we are young boys, it's drilled in us that we are men. Man up! Stop acting like a baby! Big boys don't cry! In fact, we are just trying to be little boys and experience life as a kid. We are encouraged to be tough and discouraged from being in touch with our emotions. Straighten up your face! I better not see any tears! If you cry, I'm going to give you something to cry about! These words come from women and men alike.

In many cases, we are forced to be the man of the house at a young age because a lot of African American households are headed by single mothers. More specifically, 94% of single parent households in the African American community are headed by single mothers. So, we become the protector, the covering, the husband, the boyfriend, the big brother (even if we're younger than our siblings), the worker and so much more. But most times, we aren't taught to be any of those things. That's not to say that we don't learn to do the best we can and in most cases, we don't mind serving in those roles because most men need to feel needed. But when do young boys in these situations get to be boys?

It's at this point that most boys begin wearing the mask...you know, the one that hides the tears...and feelings...and emotions...and pains...and wants...and desires...and disappointments... We've already established that we can't cry because tears for a boy is a sign of weakness. Isn't that what they say? We can't adequately address why we feel abandoned because our fathers are nowhere to be found.

Faced with abandonment issues... a lot of times crying

out for fathers… or rebelling… or trying to be the man of the house without the proper knowledge of what a man is and does… some boys are simply expected to be something or someone we've never seen.

Then, when faced with real men issues, we are held to a standard that we really weren't prepared to maintain. So we're already behind the 8 ball and expected to carry the load. As we get older, the burden increases. More responsibilities come and our on-the-job training hasn't caught up to the demand of us being a man. We get into relationships and must now be the husband to our wives, again expected to be something many never saw, raise children, including young boys to be different than we were without the tools to do so. But who do we go to to talk about it? Remember, if you complain, you are weak. If you talk about it, you're weak. Man up, they say!

So we don't talk about it…to anyone. We bottle it up inside until it boils over and spews its venom on anyone in close proximity. Usually, it's in the form of aggression against other men or sexual extrovertist behaviors with women on the other end of the spectrum. And if you factor in other variables such as child abuse; molestation and rape; living in poverty; negative environments and people; abandonment issues; mental illnesses; and the like, you have a recipe for disaster where no one is safe from the poison.

Most African American families follow a "we don't discuss what happens in this house" mentality, whether it's verbalized that way or it's known by a look and/or family history. And the stigma of counseling and therapy in the black community further complicates the struggle to overcome this dynamic.

So, in this project, there are nine men and visionary Michelle S. Lovett, who are willing to become vulnerable and share their stories about their pain, inadequacies, mistakes, and processes to help others move toward healing and develop their character. After hearing some of the men discuss their stories, I was excited about what this book would mean to so many people. And when Michelle invited me to write this foreword, I was more than willing because I could relate to many of their plights. I wanted to join their efforts to remove the masks, become vulnerable, continue the healing progress and continue to build character, as we seek to be blessings to others.

Everyone who knows me knows I am nonconfrontational. I try my best to avoid confrontation for myself and between others because I've seen so many situations that escalated so fast that life-changing results followed... whether that was jail, death, divorce, broken relationship, etc. Don't get me wrong. I know that confrontation is necessary at times, but I tend to think of the potential negative outcomes because of what I witnessed. One day, when I was probably 12 or 13, I was forced into a confrontation with a boy who bullied me. I was always one of the smallest kids in any circle I was in and by me being nonconfrontational, I was an easy target. But on this day, the bully was bothering my younger cousin on the sidewalk in front of my grandmother's house. My protector instinct kicked in. I crashed through the front door of the house and made a beeline right to the same boy who teased me about my name and chased me home from school on numerous occasions. But someone I loved was in trouble and needed me.

I reached him and threw him off my cousin with all the strength that abandonment issues, being the family protector, and lack of positive role models in my life provided me in that moment. I put him in a headlock and squeezed and yelled for someone to come get me off him because I knew that I wasn't going to let loose until he stopped moving. Fortunately for him and for me, my aunt (the same one who taught me how to defend myself against bullies like him) finally ran out the house and saved him...I mean us. I might have still had him in the headlock some 35 years later. And yes, I was crying the entire time because I was out of character and it scared me. It showed me what I was capable of doing out of fear, anger and pain. And I didn't like it.

Years later, my mother in-law said she feared the person/people I'd unleash my wrath on because she saw how much I was still holding inside dating back to my youth. She encouraged me tap into the parts of me I still kept hidden behind the mask, even though I had made some strides in developing my real character and identity. But the truth of the matter was I didn't want to deal with it because it would resurrect the pains and emotions that I was always encouraged to keep buried.

When I was young, I didn't talk about the pain I was feeling inside, even though I knew I could talk to my mother about anything. Occasionally, I would write about it, but even then some things I never shared with anyone because I didn't want to appear weak or weird. So like many young boys, I began wearing the mask. I began becoming what others wanted me or expected of me. I began masking my pain and acting like I was all right, when in fact, I was hurting and crying out for love, for attention, for compassion, and for understanding. But how could my mother, my aunts, my grandmother, and my female cousins who basically raised me, know what it was like to be a young boy with so much pressure from all these women... and the pressure from society which had its own labels (mainly negative ones) of me as a young black male. The few men in my family and the ones in my neighborhood didn't provide many positive examples for me either. I couldn't go to them for advice. I felt like I was on an island by myself. I would have to figure some things out for myself while trying to live up to the massive expectations because to many, I *was* different.

Because of what I saw drugs and alcohol do in my family and community, they never became my vices like they did for many boys and men who struggled to live up to expectations placed on them. Many attempted to drown their pain in alcohol or get high to escape the reality of what they were experiencing. For me, I found an escape and comfort in the arms of girls and women, including my older cousin's friends and my mother's friends. I lost my virginity when I was 10 or 11. But many of my encounters weren't related to sex. I found myself needing to be with women...to protect them...to cover them...to love them because so many were crying out to be loved. The women in my family taught me how to talk to a lady and how to treat a lady. They taught me to respect a lady and how to love a lady... based on what they wanted and expected and often missed from the men in their lives. So like everything else, that was the basis for my education because I didn't have a male figure around me taking me under his wing.

The problem was I felt like I had to be that for too many women, so much so that a friend of mine called me Captain Save a Hoe! I wasn't necessarily trying to save all of them but just like I came to the rescue of my cousin and I was used to being that for most of the females in my family, I saw other females in the same light. But I love hard, which means you become vulnerable... which means you have a greater propensity to get hurt.

My first real girlfriend, my first love, broke my heart. My second love broke my heart, too. So not only did I continue to wear the mask of a boy in pain because of his childhood issues, now, I was wearing body armor to try to prevent my heart from being crushed again. By the time I got married, I was wounded, bruised inside and trying to hide it behind the mask and armor. But because I always knew that I wanted to be married, I thought everything would be great when we said, "I do". But here I was again, stepping into the role of husband and father, roles I had no idea about because I didn't have those examples around me as a child and wasn't taught what to expect. And my wife, who had an example of a marriage with her parents, had expectations all her own. There were some learning and growing that needed to take place. But they came with their own issues and challenges that found us on a roller coaster journey, often fighting the proverbial uphill battle. I know I am not perfect so I take some responsibility for some of our struggles in my marriage because as a grown man, I was still dealing with young boy issues that were eroding the inside of my being. And as I wrote in one of my books, *Devil in the Mirror*, I was willing to take a long, hard look at myself, be honest with myself and determine that I wanted to be better for me first and then I could be better for my wife, my children, my extended family, friends and any other relationship that needed me to be whole. I overcame that depression and vowed to always stay in a process of improving. As I often say, "Growing things live and living things grow."

So I can appreciate the pain of the men who contributed to this project and the men all over the world who still need healing, even in their senior years. This book is not just for us; it's for women, too. These stories invite women into a secret place of men's pain, where our character growth has been stunted for years from unresolved issues. Maybe you will look at your husband a little differently after reading this book. Maybe you will treat your son a little differently. Maybe you will identify your own pain and allow that to build your character, too.

My prayer is that we continue to build one another rather than tear one another down as society wants. It's not an impossible task. But we must all start with ourselves. As men, we must shed the macho image and bravado and become vulnerable to overcome some of the deep-seeded issues that have been growing inside of us for years. Yes, being vulnerable exposes us to the possibility of even more pains, but it also opens us up to the greatest possible emotions because we have released the toxins. For many, today will be the day our pain becomes our character.

C. Nathaniel Brown
Founder/CEO
Expected End Entertainment

C. Nathaniel Brown is an award-winning writer, filmmaker, publisher and coach. A multiple bestselling author of 13 books, he is founder and CEO of Expected End Entertainment, a full service media and entertainment company based in Atlanta. The company's mission is to entertain, educate and empower through various services that include film, television, book publishing and writer coaching to name a few. The Baltimore native's personal mission is to help people dream bigger, live their dreams and impact their world. One of his goals is to help 10,000 writers to become published. He has also written, produced and/or directed more than 30 films and mentors up-and-coming actors, screenplay writers, producers and directors.

Peace & Blessings Always!

Jer. 29:11

x

CHAPTER 1

GOD HAD A PLAN
Michelle S. Lovett, Curator

Pain is a distressing feeling often caused by intense or damaging stimuli. The International Association for the Study of Pain's widely used definition defines pain as "an unpleasant sensory". Volume 2 of *Life, Love & Lockup: My Pain Became My Character*, focuses on different causes and effects of deeply rooted pain, disease, discomfort, disgust, dishonor and disappointment we all can have. Plus, what caused my shift to occur.

I came into the world with a long list of medical issues and a well-defined battle ahead of me. But since birth, I have been determined to win. Despite doctors' conversations, failed medical treatments, heart murmurs, naysayers and unbelievers, GOD HAD A PLAN! Since entering my mother's womb, I have had an anointing and covering on my life. We are all placed on this earth for a purpose. I've always been a student and realized we will always have work to do, which has assisted me on my journey. Tests offer testimonies. Sometimes, observation leads to passing judgment, however in most cases you receive false reads! Based on my life experiences, many find it hard to believe that 43 years later, I'm still here. Read Volume 1 of *Life, Love & Lockup*, my biography or reference www.lifeloveandlockup.com for all the details of what I've been through. I can only tell you my story.

Discomfort

My mother already had four children (Gloria, Emmanuel, Jackie and Donna), and my father had one son (Tommy), before they got married. They both wanted a child together. My mother and father already experienced two miscarriages before conceiving me. Mentally, mom became locked up. Thinking about having another child was impossible. Dad and mom's spiritual capacity was being tested. God whispered and said "This flower will bloom!" Bennie and Gloria was chosen to receive the blueprint. They received the formula because God knew they were strong enough for the road ahead. My mother and father were blessed with a child September 7, 1976, and named her Michelle Shawn Lovett.

Growing up in a blended family naturally creates "blended family chronicles". Most times, bringing everyone together can cause discomfort, especially when one sibling is used to being the baby for a long time and another child is born. Often, this can formulate slight pain or embarrassment. Here's a great example: my sister Donna (RIP) was considered the baby girl for 13 years, until my mother and father had me. Then all hell broke loose. My parents would wake up to me screaming nightly because Donna would be pinching me. The transformation for her was too great. Wait, here's the kicker. Throughout life she was one of my personal protectors. We were spaced out in age but close in real life. I wanted to go everywhere and do everything she did. She was the popular, outgoing, caring, loving, giving, don't get it twisted type. I modeled behind her in many areas. For example, Donna was the first African American dance line captain for Homestead Senior High School, and I was the first Baby Bronco Mascot. When I went to high school, I was placed in magnet schools (Southwood Middle and New World of Fine Arts Montessori schools) for drama and singing. By the time I reached 10th grade, my sister convinced my parents to allow me to attend Homestead Senior just so I could be captain of the dance line and it happened by my junior year.

Another example of discomfort was my oldest sister's child is two years older than me. I'm his aunt but him calling me Auntie Michelle was out of the question. I grew up as his little sister. My sister Gloria assisted my mother with me. She took care of me many times because my mother was nervous, often to even hold me as a result of my weight and health issues. Plus, my mother dealt with postpartum depression.

Although my father was not my siblings' biological father, one rule in our family was never refer to anyone as step- anything. Mom would say, "Ain't nobody stepped on nobody!" So, we all were treated equally. In fact, my dad adopted Donna and gave her his last name (Donna Lovett).

Many times, I felt isolated from other family members and that my siblings even treated me differently because I was our parents only biological child. Everyone considered me spoiled and I get it. However, one must consider both the time and medical issues I had experienced, as reasons for the different treatment. By the time I entered into this world, my parents were financially on another level. I didn't grow up like most of my siblings because my parents had me at a later age in their lives. Secondly, another challenge I was faced with derived from me being blessed to grow up in a two-parent home. To most that grew up around me in Dade County, having this structure in the home seemed far-fetched.

Both of my parents were very active in my life. My mother worked and retired as a migrant paraprofessional. She would take care of home and my wellbeing. My father was always working, either in his profession, building our family empire, the community or church. He retired from the Air Force after serving over 23 years. He also retired from

Florida City as chief code enforcer, worked multiple side jobs, owned different commercial and residential properties, a limousine service and a store. Truly, hustle is a part of my DNA. At an early age, I worked on different voting campaigns, at the daycare center or babysitting, and for Miami Subs restaurant in the 10th grade, in addition to being active in school, church, the community and learning about our family's businesses. There were many other things my parents, church members, receiving a great education and life experiences taught me or was instilled in me growing up. I implement a lot of them daily in my life.

Disease

As a child, I was called ugly and weird most of the time because of my health conditions. I faced many physical challenges, unable to gain weight, hair loss, eczema destroyed my skin and forced to wear glasses. At birth, I was diagnosed with different allergies to certain foods and several items. Twice a week, I had to get allergy shots and attend doctor appointments, monitoring my asthma and other health conditions. If that wasn't bad enough, I received my menstrual cycle at the age of 9. I wasn't prepared or educated on what was happening to my body. From Day 1, I experienced complications. Over a period of time, the cramps and pain became unbearable. In 1999, doctors performed a surgery in hopes of suppressing some pain, which initially went away but quickly returned. Doctors found fibroids and cysts on my ovaries. Two laparoscopies and a myomectomy were performed to remove everything in 2001. In 2002, I tried again to get pregnant but was unsuccessful after years of trying. Have I ever gotten pregnant? I divulge that information in Volume 3. Just know that God blesses all my mother's daughters with two children. Was I really suffering from endometriosis or was it lupus or both? Why wasn't I tested for lupus earlier in my life? It all puzzles me. However, stay tuned. I'm actively researching for answers. But I also understand that I had to go through because helping others is part of my mission. So far, I realized following holistic regimens work better than pharmaceutical medicines. Please check my website out at memeallover.tavalifestyle.com/

In 2005, heavy stress came from every angle and it all seemed too much. Fibroids returned causing me to have several other surgeries. Then I was diagnosed with endometriosis. Doctors used several medications and treatments, even hormone replacement (Lupron and birth control) in hopes of shrinking the endometriosis. In 2006, things began to turn around.

Disappointment

June 2005, I received a phone call that seemed like a nightmare. My family notified me that my father was diagnosed with prostate cancer. In 2006, he initiated his healing process by utilizing holistic measures. I tried to come to grips with it all. However, things would never process. I leaned heavily on God for strength. I'm happy that my parents taught and showed me the power of prayer. Fourteen years later, my father is still living and has broken his silence.

My father breaking his silence on his medical issues is huge to me because of the private nature of how we were brought up. However, I completely agree with my father on this because *Life, Love & Lockup* is based on individuals' truths and real testimonials. The book and documentary are shared with the world in hopes of assisting others cope with difficult life circumstances while providing some resolution.

Later in 2006, I was promoted on my job. My promotion required me to travel significantly. I had to work more. My husband had lost his high paying job, after going through depression following the death of his grandmother. He wasn't bringing in the finances we were accustomed to. With me being away working all the time, our marriage began to take a turn for the worse. Everything started becoming an issue, including the old saying, "Romance without finance, becomes a nuisance". To add insult to injury, I struggled with different things such as my sickness, the thought of my dad losing his fight to cancer, and the thought of never being able to bless my husband with a child to call our own. I was so afraid but walked around as if I was strong. However, I was falling apart. In 2007, we separated. I moved to Atlanta after being promoted on my job again. My life totally changed. I was scared but determined to press through it all.

In 2008, I was faced with yet another medical trauma. Doctors called me and said the endometriosis had spread plus some fibroids and cysts had returned and it was best to have my left fallopian tube removed. My mom came to support me throughout the process as always. She whispered, "Chell, be done with it. Have a hysterectomy. I'm tired of you going through all this. I will probably be gone to heaven soon." I screamed, "GURLLL STOP!" In July 2009, after attending my niece's wedding, I found myself standing in my closet as my body went limp and veins begin to drain. Moments later, I received the call that forever changed my life. "Michelle, come to South Fulton Hospital now!" I took my time as my sisters' kept rushing me. I realized my body reactions was a sign that Mom was leaving.

Two days before my mother went into a coma, she told me how proud she was of me. I was the only daughter to complete college. I had a sophisticated career and she made sure I was set for life no matter what. Even writing this, I still hurt because I feel she taken too soon. I couldn't believe the night I was supposed to be there sitting and monitoring my mom, she sent me home to be with my sister who wasn't feeling well. My mother knew I couldn't handle her passing in my presence. God gave that assignment to Dad. Mom was in a coma but we still communicating. She went to heaven once I told her I wasn't mad if she had to go and that I would be ok.

I wasn't ok. I often think about how I, the baby, assisted in planning my mother's funeral, bought her dressing and even spoke at the funeral. Daily, I walked with the full armor of God, praying without ceasing.

After my mother died, my husband and I tried to reconcile our relationship in 2009 but was unsuccessful. We both realized we were trying to reconcile for all the wrong reasons, mainly because my mom had always told us to take care of each other and never just throw in the towel.

Eight months later, I became extremely ill, even needing blood transfusions (that I refused). So, I was forced to have a total hysterectomy. My entire life changed overnight. Before I could completely heal, my dad's new girlfriend called and said one of my brothers had transitioned. The first thing I thought was, "Why are you calling me and why isn't my dad calling?" I couldn't believe this woman, whom I barely knew, was on the phone telling me my brother had died. Then I prayed and God shifted my thinking. Satan wanted my attention on the woman but my attention needed to be on what really transpired with my brother. I went to my brother's home and quickly figured something out. I was extremely angry. What was I going to do? Who could I turn to? Everyone knew what really happened. That was the most hurtful part of it all because it was nothing anybody could do. I had experienced back-to-back deaths of my mother (2009) and brother (2010) and the lost possibility to bear children. Prescription drugs, alcohol and marijuana became my best friends. I was doing anything to numb the pain.

In 2011, I started dating, fell in love and three months later, he became incarcerated. However, we had an interesting eight-year, complicated relationship. Later that same year, the pain kept knocking on my door. I was diagnosed with fibromyalgia. In 2012, doctors ran several tests and different physicians gave opinions, confirming the diagnosis of Lupus.

While I battled Lupus, I left the corporate world and opened my own entertainment company. I was adjusting to Daddy getting remarried and battling a heavy addiction to pharmaceutical drugs and an array of other things. I literally gave up on LIFE, shut LOVE out and became LOCKED UP!

Dishonor, Disgust & Betrayal

In 2013, the man I fell in love with was released from prison. He was ready to get married but I was still legally married to my husband for multiple reasons. So later that year, I got divorced from my husband. But how could I divorce my husband only to endure an unhealthy, violent, abusive, controlling, manipulative relationship? I felt like I should have honored my vows a little more, prayed and got through things. After being with my new man during two prison bids, visiting weekly and every holiday, and sending him money, he became my life. Nothing or no one else mattered. I went hard, he made me feel special but that's because I was in a real dark space when I met him. I dealt with infidelity, deceit, disrespect, etc. Most things I caught on to but his good (at the time) outweighed his bad. Plus, the Percocet, Ambien, and Xanax kept me sleeping and calm. I experienced blow after blow... literally sometimes. In the end, I realized hurt people hurt others. He hurt me and I further hurt myself by remaining.

Be careful because whatever you sow, that you shall also reap. I ended up assisting him with his children while he was in another relationship. Most would call me stupid but the kids considered me an angel. (I am writing more on this situation in my upcoming book so stay close for that.)

My father and I have always been best friends. We never kept secrets and always had an unbreakable bond. When he remarried, we weren't really talking much. I couldn't understand how he could remarry so quickly. I was trying to process my dad's total transformation, my brother's death, feeling I was betrayed, and our family falling apart. Regular family events slowly disappearing along with family visits. Disconnect and discomfort were alive and well in our family. The streets were talking but our teachings kept us quiet. I crawled into a dark hole, cut off from everyone and started my own family. Normally that would have been fine if the mate was ready. Well, he wasn't. I felt all alone so I increased my meds trying to escape from everything.

Late in 2016, my lupus became extremely aggressive. Doctors gave me six months to live. I started eating clean, kicked the drugs, and began fasting and praying. A year later, my lupus went into remission. I truly believe my survival was God's divine order. But it took some time for me to get a full understanding of what God was doing.

Everything I stood for, I fell for. The different shifts that took place in my life, mentally, physically, spiritually and even literally, all led me to become locked up! Everything overwhelming. I slipped into a dark place, a deep depression. I couldn't see any light. It caused me to have low self-esteem, I forgot who I really was, and more importantly, whose I was (God's). Many times, I even questioned why was I still living?

My Pain Became My Character

Satan's plan didn't work. I went to sleep and fell into a coma but before they could pull the plug, God opened my eyes. I almost let go but God kept me. In the nick of time, God decided to give me another chance. My prayer is that everyone will understand that in life, a little rain must fall. However, hold on. Better days are coming! I'm no longer locked up. Thank God, I'm free! No more chains holding me! I looked at my trials, sickness and even death and said, "LET GO OF ME!" I recognize the order of God. Things, people and situations that were meant to destroy me, actually became my character.

Michelle S. Lovett is a bestselling author, publisher, entrepreneur, and curator coach. Born in Homestead, Florida, to Bennie and Gloria Lovett, she has always had a passion for pursuing her dreams while helping others achieve theirs. An accomplished actor of stage, television and film, Michelle enjoys spending quality time with family and friends and challenging herself to grow in every area of her life. She created the *Life, Love & Lockup* series to create opportunities for herself and others to receive the healing they need. After overcoming several of her own challenges in her life, Michelle is determined to help others win. *(See extended bio on page 101.)*

CHAPTER 2

THE MAKING OF A BETTER MAN
James T. Thompson

"Pain is not always because of the devil. It can be God's motivation for you to see the path made for you."

I stepped out the car, and the smell of the neighborhood awakened memories I had forgotten. The memories of the yells, the menacing stares, the lashes with the belt, all came back. The only choice was to stay with my father's mother; he would not let me stay with my maternal grandmother. As I got closer to the building, the memories kept coming back… from that building and other locations: Eastern Parkway, where he kicked me for walking slow with the groceries; Madison Avenue, where he beat me for getting dressed because I thought he would give permission to go on a day trip with my cousins; and Woman's Hospital, where he jumped at my mother while she lay in the hospital bed. I wondered if I had made the right decision to come there. I stood in front of the building that he lived in. Should I go back to the car and continue my life as it had been, or do I go face my father, the man I had not seen in 33 years?

You may wonder how I got to this point in my life? Let's visit some of my past, and then we will come back to this point. I was born in Brooklyn, NY, at Brooklyn Jewish Hospital on September 29, 1967. My little sister was born two years after me. There were some very trying times. I witnessed things that a kid should not witness, but in those days many of us did. Out of respect for my mother, I will not give details on some of those times, but I will say I witnessed and heard things that should not be said or done by any man to the woman he loves.

With the help of my mother's parents, we were able to escape those times in New York and move to North Carolina for a fresh start. In the initial weeks and months, I longed for my father. I would sometimes lay awake waiting for him to show up and take us back to New York. Some of those nights I cried because he never showed. As the months and years went past, I acquainted myself with the fact that he was not coming. I then recognized my hero, my mother. She is the ROCK. All boys want their dads to be the hero, but seeing her do what she was doing, she took the title. We never needed for anything. Well, actually, we did, but she made it feel as if we had everything that we could ever want. During this time, I developed an 'us against the world' type of mentality. It wasn't in a militant kind of way, but in a way that would make my mother proud. Anyone that encountered me, I wanted to leave an impression that would make them give my mother all the respect in the world. I wanted to be the most courteous, respectful young man that I could be to make sure that the light shined on her in a way that no light shined. This has stuck with me for life. It has become me. So, this is how my pain helped shape my character.

As life went on, I stayed true to the character I wanted to be, the good kid, good guy that was raised the right way so that my mother would always be looked upon as doing it right, even though she did it alone. She worked many jobs, some at night, but she still introduced church to my sister and me. We learned about God, the belief, and prayer at Saint Paul Freewill Baptist Church. I grew up with a calmness, a confidence that was born from the pain I had endured of feeling neglected by my father. I remember seeing talk shows on television, when serial killers or rapists used the abuse they endured growing up as reasons/excuses for the crimes they committed. I never wanted anyone to be able to use my upbringing/the absence of my father as reason for something I did. So, I found role models. I looked up to some older dudes, who called themselves the Funky Grannies... guys like Johnny Hargrove, Dennis Humphrey, Michael Thomas and Earl Cummings to name a few. I was able to see how a man should be. Again, my pain was shaping my character.

Growing up 'down south' (as New Yorkers call it) was interesting. After the hustle and flow of New York City, the calmness and easiness of Richlands, NC, was welcomed. I learned about hard work. First, I saw my mother doing it. Second, I recognized that if I wanted things, I also needed to do it. This also kept me from asking for things from my mother. I was a solid student, played sports and was having the usual childhood. I had pretty much blocked out any thoughts of my father. The congratulations and pats on the back that most kids got from their fathers, I got from the old heads in the neighborhood. These men will probably never know how much they helped, but this also helped shape me into the man I am today.

I graduated from Richlands High School and sports was my thing. I had college opportunities, but without the understanding of what went on with athletic scholarships, I decided to join the U.S. Army. You see, I never wanted to be a burden on my mother. I watched her do what she did to make sure my little sister and I had what we needed. She still had my little sister to take care of, so I did not want to have to bother her for money while in college. The pain was shaping my character.

I enlisted in the Army ready for life. I served at Ft. Ord, Calif., and in Frankfurt, Germany. I lived the life of a soldier and had good times and bad times. However, I was still that mild-mannered guy that everyone got along with. I even got married at the young age of 19. Once my marriage didn't work out, I found myself dating multiple women, sabotaging any real relationship I got in. While I was in Germany, I was playing games with women, sometimes dating six at a time. Some female friends of mine said I was the nicest womanizer they knew. Tell me, how does those character traits go together? I have no idea. I was discharged in 1991 and was ready for life on the outside as a regular citizen.

My first real job as a grown man was as a Correctional Officer in North Carolina. I really enjoyed the job. I was around a lot of street dudes, so I was able to relate because of my connections to New York. I was still able to be the person I wanted to be - likeable, relatable, respectful and helpful. I had meaningful conversations with inmates daily. This is when I realized that my life experiences might help others. I worked with youth and adult offenders. I met killers, drug dealers and rapists. Some of these men had some of the same abusive moments that I had in their early years. They were using those situations as reasons or excuses for what they had done. I spoke to them, pushing them to release this way of thinking. Holding on to that excuse will give them a green light, subconsciously, to continue down the wrong path.

Fast forward 20 years. I am in Atlanta, on my way to work and that moment happened. It was a Wednesday, and I was supposed to be at work at 8:30 that morning. Instead, I called in saying I would be a little late. Understand, if I was at work on time that day, the moment that I feel changed my life may not have happened. There was a show on the radio highlighting children of abusive relationships. I was sitting at the light and then heard this from a caller: He was a survivor of an abusive parental relationship. His father abused him, and his mother did, too, physically and verbally, and he felt it may be the reason he was having problems sustaining a long healthy relationship. He was asked if he was abusive to his mate and he said it was the exact opposite. He was not, but he always found a way to end his relationships.

That stuck to me. I mean, it stuck to me all that day. The next day, I checked on my benefits and recognized I had three free visits to counseling services. I figured, why not take advantage of this? I felt fine, like my life was going well. However, God was pushing me. He was showing me that there was something missing. He was all over me on this day. Being late was not the devil, it was God making sure I received the message through the radio.

After setting my appointment, I really started thinking about my life. I felt great. I was making good money, I was able to take care of my son, and I was traveling when I wanted to. I mean life was pretty good. One thing that was missing was that one woman that would make me feel complete. Now, this had nothing to do with the ladies I had dated. I dated some good women who were good looking, educated, financially secure, and confident. The thing is I could not think of anything that any of them did so wrong to me that we had to break up. So, as the gentleman on the show mentioned, I was figuring out ways to sabotage these relationships. I really thought back. It was so real. I started calling some of the ladies I had dated in the past to apologize.

I go through my three visits, and as I figured, the

absence of my father had such an effect on me. A positive effect, but also an underlying negative one. I had questions that I needed to be answered. The answers may not be something that could be given to me from a distance. Maybe it would be something I needed to see. So, I started planning a trip to New York to see my father.

I knew it was going to be a difficult task. I had not been back to New York in years. I had family there, but no one that I felt comfortable enough to ask if I could stay with them. I finally reached out to a family member, and he said I could stay with him. The night before I was scheduled to fly to New York, there was heavy rain in the New York area, which caused my cousin's apartment to flood. My trip was going to have to be postponed. At that moment, I decided that this might not be what I should be doing. I decided not to do it. You know what they say... "When you think you know what you are going to do, God steps in and shows you the truth."

But I eventually make it to New York. I am walking to the building my father lived in. I get off the elevator on his floor. As I walk towards his door, I was nervous. My mind was all over the place. I knock. Would I get angry at the sight of him? Would I lash out? Would I reach out to hug him? I knock again. No answer. I knock a third time and again, no answer. A neighbor steps out, and tells me that my father was not at home, that he had gone to get his dreads treated. The first thing I thought was, "Dreads?" It really had been that long since I had seen him. I asked the neighbor if she knew where he had gone, thinking I could drive to whatever salon he had gone to. I was full speed ahead. I needed to get this done. She gave me a look and then I realized what I had asked. I was standing in the hallway of Pink Houses, a dangerous area in East New York that was known for violence. Why would she give me his location? I told her I was his son. Her eyes widened, and she asked if I was Tyrone Jr. She said, "He talks about you all the time." Now that caught me off guard. He had been speaking about me? I did not expect that at all.

She told me he had gone over to Bedford Stuyvesant. So, I figured I would go visit some others and then come back. Before I got back on the elevator, it seemed as if a weight was lifted off me, but it was more of a break from the nerves. I stepped off the elevator, out of the building, and then I heard a voice to my left. I looked and there he was... my father, who I had not laid eyes on in 33 years. We locked eyes and it seemed as if I lost rhythm in my breathing. He leaned his head to the side and said, "Junior?" I replied, "Yeah. 'Sup Pops." We just looked at each other. Then finally approached and hugged. What I had prepared for was upon me and I was at a loss for words. Saying it was awkward is an understatement.

So, we made our way back up to the apartment. Once inside, I wondered what to say. Do I ask how he has been? I mean, did I care? Do I tell him how I waited for him to show up when I was a kid? What should the first words be? Honestly, I can't tell you how it started. What I can tell you is that when I stepped into the apartment, memories flooded me. My father was staying in the same apartment that my grandmother stayed in when I was a kid. I know we talked, and I was on edge the entire time. I was worried about saying something that would make him say the wrong thing and trigger the anger I had inside. He was having drinks plus altering his mind in other ways. Then, the moment happened. It was a reminder that the God I serve is a good God. As we were having conversations about life, he kept bringing up things about the past. It was as if he was trying to make my mother out to be the bad person. It was as if he was trying to give me reasons to excuse his behavior. I was doing all I could to remain in a positive mental space... mainly smiling and laughing.

Then to add to my struggles, he kept calling my mother out of her name, using words like broad or bitch. He and I had spoken on the phone before this trip and he was able to say some things and all I could do is ask for him not to. Now that I was in front of him, I told him, "You are not going to keep referring to my mother out of her name! You will address her with the respect she has deserves!" He said he was from New York and this is just how men from New York spoke. I told him I was also from New York, and I knew how to change my vocabulary in the presence of women. He did not like that at all. He stood up, not really towering over me, but I was sitting so he was looking down at me. I looked up and I knew if I stood up, there was going to be a real problem. You see, there was a window near, and we were on the 6th floor. All the anger, the resentment, the memories of seeing my mother struggle to make sure my sister and I were raised with pleasantries swirled inside of me. I knew that if I had stood up, it would all boil over and I was going to push him out that window. So, I sat still, and I prayed as I took deep breaths. He then sad, "I can respect that, son." That was the moment. I didn't know when it would come, but that was it. I knew God had me. And again, it showed how my pain had become my character.

I visited with my father's other family members. I found myself hiding my emotions. So many of my family members kept speaking about how my father had some great kids, had done such a good job with me, and how much I reminded them of him. Then someone said, Betty, my mother, should not have taken us away from him. That statement bothered me but I smiled and said nothing. I hugged necks and welcomed them back into my life. Again, my God is great, and this shows how my pain had become my character.

After this visit, I realized the strength of my character. I realized that the absence of my father and the underlying pain may have actually made me a better man. How can that be? I will never know who I would have been with him in my life because he was not there. Right now, I know who I am. I am a man, a brother, a son, a friend and I am also a father. Being a father means a lot to me because of the absence of mine. My son did not grow up in the same house as me, but I made sure to be close. I wanted to show my son the importance of the communication between father and son. So, me and my father having a relationship was important for my own relationship with my son. I figured I need him to meet my father so that he could see that I practiced what I preached. You guessed it, I arranged for my son and I to go and see my father, his grandfather, on Father's Day.

If you are wondering whether reconnecting with my father has had any effect on my life, I will tell you that I really feel complete! I see things differently. Life is more enjoyable. I have opened myself up for love, which makes loving easier. I have been released from the lockup of my emotional turmoil. Today, my father and I have a pretty good relationship. It is still growing. Each time I visit, there are more answers to the questions I have always had. He has apologized for some things and given some reasons for others. But he has admitted that the reasons were mostly because of himself.

Because of the pain I endured as a young man, it molded me to kick the stereotype. I was not going to be the one who did the wrong thing and let growing up in a single parent household be the narrative.

I am humble, respectful, courteous, passionate, accountable, and relatable because of my pain. My pain became my character.

James T. Thompson is a U.S. Army veteran who served from 1985-1991. After the military, he became a correctional officer in North Carolina. A Brooklyn, New York native who calls Richlands, North Carolina, home, he enjoys sharing his experiences with others. James, or JT as he is affectionately called, moved to Atlanta in 1994 with an eye on a good time. He worked as a collections specialist before moving on to the sales arena. He then ventured into the entertainment industry at the age of 48 to motivate others. James lives by the motto: "The biggest room in the world is the room for improvement." He strives to improve as a father, friend, son, brother and man.

CHAPTER 3

THE CHURCH BOY/LIVE AGAIN
Dominique Marquie Releford

Most people who know me would describe me as the "church boy", the one who comes from the perfect first family. But my story goes much deeper than meets the eye. I was born Dominique Marquie Releford in Goppingen, Germany. You can say that I'm an army brat. We stayed in Germany until I was about 3 years old. They said when I moved here, I couldn't speak a bit of English, but I am glad that eventually I learned.

We were the perfect family, my mom, dad and I. We were dedicated to my grandfather's church, where my mom, after pastoring a church in Germany, was a dedicated youth pastor and my dad a faithful deacon. I remember going to church every Sunday and almost every day during the week. There was always some revival or some sort of program going on at the church. So, being involved in ministry became natural. I was active in the choir, on the praise team and played the drums and keyboard. I was surrounded by musicians and preachers, so it was inevitable that I would follow suit in some capacity.

I truly enjoyed church. I was a happy kid, always fun, loving, and things were good. That was until I experienced a situation that would change my life forever. You see, right when I became an adolescent, I was raped. It is one thing to be assaulted by someone of the opposite sex, but being a man and being violated by another man, was hurtful and humiliating. Because of the shame, I kept it to myself. This is when my nightmares began. I would have nightmares, reliving the trauma that I experienced. I relived it over and over again. I walked around with the secret for a while, until one day my parents got a devastating call. I will never forget my mother running into my room in tears, yelling, "Why didn't you tell me? Why didn't you tell me you were raped?" My rapist had the guts to call my mom and tell her, "While you were protecting everyone else's children, I raped your son." All the emotions from that day came flooding back to my mind. The hurt, the embarrassment, guilt, the shame. Such a traumatic experience for a young boy. Now, I had to look my parents in the face and admit that I was raped, by a man whom I couldn't fight off. That happy little boy that was so outgoing became bitter and angry. The family that was thought to be perfect became divided. Everything was beginning to change for the worse.

I walked around with feelings of anger, fear and bitterness weighing me down. I was living in a world of silent frustration. Being that my family was a well-known family of preachers, news about what happened to me traveled fast. To my surprise, instead of the church embracing me, they caused more wounds. Any time I walked past a crowd, I would hear whispers, "You know that's the preacher's son that had sex with a man." I was embarrassed and hurt. I will admit that experience will confuse someone about their sexuality. I remember visiting churches in the area and various preachers would want to prophesy to me and tell me in front of big congregations to stop living a lie and admit that I was a homosexual and come out of my homosexual lifestyle.

As the news continued to spread, more and more people joined the bandwagon. Preachers would go as far as to preach sermons about me when they visited our church. They would say that I wasn't raped, and I wanted it. This not only came from church members who knew me all my life, but from family members as well. How could people in the church be so cruel? If they really had the Holy Ghost, if they really had the spirit of Christ, then why couldn't they see the mental and emotional anguish I was in. So, to prove my masculinity, I began to sleep with every girl in which I came in contact. That included women that were much older than me, just to prove to everyone - and myself - that I was a real man.

While visiting my aunt in New York, I met this young lady who attended her church. Eventually, we developed a relationship and she moved to Georgia with me. We got our own place together and not long after, I found out she was pregnant. We were in love, or at least I was at the time. I made the decision to pop the question. She said yes. However, one day on the way to work, I received a call asking me had I seen her. Being that she was pregnant and was my soon-to-be wife, I was worried. No one had seen her. I was frantic. Later that day, I found out that she left work and went back to her hometown in New York. The mother of my first child had abandoned me. She left with no explanation or reason. I was completely devastated and confused. Everything seemed to be going so well. I had planned to spend my life with this woman, and she left me. To this day, I still don't know what made her leave.

The pain of missing out on all the special moments of watching my child grow up remains. I missed her first steps and first words. It hurts because I was robbed of these moments. And then to be called a deadbeat dad when you desired to be in your child's life, hurts even more. The pain is indescribable. All you want is to be a part of her life and the mother won't allow it. Some will never understand the pain of having to watch your daughter grow up through pictures, Facebook or through family members who kept in contact with her. It was always the worst for me. Father's Day was always a struggle for me. It was hard watching other men with their daughters. I would become angry and bitter. I hated that they could see their daughter and I couldn't see mine. When she got old enough to talk on the phone, I would call, and her mom would tell me that she didn't' want to talk to me.

Before my grandfather passed, he told me that God would give me a wife and kids. The healing began after my son was born. It was truly a miracle because my wife wasn't even supposed to be able to have children, but God blessed us not with one, but two children. But let me not get ahead of myself. It was very important for me to be in all of my kids' lives because I know the pain of not having your father around. The emptiness of the divorce and separation can affect a child in ways that people don't realize.

I know you may be confused right now and probably asking how is this possible? Weren't my parent married? Let me explain. During their marriage, my father would leave us for extended periods of time. Even though things eventually started looking up towards the end of their marriage, there was a time where my parents struggled financially. As a result, we ended up having to stay with my grandparents. But my dad only dropped us off there; he didn't stay. Being a young boy and having your dad walk in and out of your life does something to you. He missed important events in my life. He wasn't there to teach me about things that a man usually shares with his son. Everything I know about being a man, I primarily got from my grandfather. My father was embarrassed because he couldn't provide for his family. So, he would live elsewhere. But to a child, I just felt abandoned and I never wanted my children to feel the hurt and pain that

I experienced.

Through everything that was going on at the time, I didn't know that a childhood friend would end up being my wife. We married on June 5, 2010. We had our own home, we were both working and making decent money. Even though my wife was told that she would never have children, she became pregnant with our son. We were so happy to be welcoming our first child to our home. One day, my wife came home and informed me that she was laid off from her job. There was no explanation. I immediately became anxious. How were we going to survive off my paycheck alone? The months ahead were hard. You don't realize how good things are until they are not. Going from everything looking up to having things change so drastically for the worst, took a toll on my family. And for the first time, we had to get on public assistance just to survive. On top of that, I had just found out my wife was pregnant with our second child, a girl.

This was also around the time that I really started preaching regularly. I ended up inheriting my paternal grandmother's church. The pressure that was on me at times seemed unbearable. My wife and I began to get into really bad arguments. Most of the time, it was about the smallest things. I was hurt, angry, confused, sad, and a constant ball of emotions...not because of my wife, but as situations continued to happen in my life, my frustrations grew more and more. Instead of talking to my wife about what I was feeling, I would just keep it all bottled up inside and be silent.

Sidebar: Remember when I said my wife was expecting a girl, my oldest child's mother also found out. Before this time, even though I couldn't see my daughter, I was financially responsible for her. Whenever she needed something for her, I would go out of my way to make sure she had it. I still do. Most of the time, my wife was the one to help send things. But it wasn't until I had a girl that my ex-wife decided to file for child support. Don't get me wrong, I believe that a man should take care of his responsibilities and if he isn't, then he deserves to be court ordered to pay child support. But when you don't allow me to see her and my name isn't on her birth certificate, it makes me feel like she only did it because I was having a girl and it was out of spite.

If things in my life weren't hectic enough, this situation added fuel to the fire. Because I was not listed as the father on the birth certificate, we had to do a DNA test and go through a long, drawn out process through the courts. Once it was determined that I was the father, which I already knew, they began to garnish my paychecks for backpay and the normal monthly obligation. After the garnishments began, my check was almost nothing. And because we were living off my check, we were forced to move out of our apartment. Here I am with a pregnant wife and a son and we were homeless.

For about four years, we bounced around from house to house, family member to family member. The entire time, I was suffering. I found myself going to church on Sunday preaching to people about trusting a God that I wasn't sure really loved or cared about me. Why would He allow my family to go through this if he really cared about us? I found myself drifting away from my faith and what I was taught. I was losing all hope.

After my daughter was born, my wife went back to work. We were able to move into our own place again. My ex-wife began allowing me to see my older daughter and talk to her on the phone. We were beginning to build a relationship. On the surface, I tried to act like everything was good, but when you don't address the demons from your past, they have a way of resurfacing. We were doing better financially, but I was still stuck in the trauma of the past. Whenever my wife and I would argue, I would revert to my parent's divorcing and ultimately get scared that we would too. I began to sleep a lot and often had nightmares about my childhood trauma, reliving all the pain. The anger that I had inside was present in my dealings with everyone. My wife couldn't even talk to me about anything without me getting angry. I became distant. And my frustrations came out when talking to my children. What was wrong with me? All the anxiety, depression, anger, abandonment by my parents, everything that I had been suppressing or ignoring came to a head in the worst way. I was a ticking time bomb and didn't even know it.

In August 2018, I had my first stroke at 33 years old. They say stress will kill you. I found that to be true. I was in the hospital for almost two weeks. I lost all feeling on my left side. I couldn't walk. I had some trouble speaking. I had difficulty remembering things. Simple things like getting dressed were difficult. My wife had to do everything for me. Because of the stroke, I wasn't able to work. I didn't have short term disability, and the money I did have soon ran out. I decided that I had to get better. I needed to go back to work to help my family. After much therapy, I regained most of the feeling on my left side and I could walk again. It may have been with a limp, but I was finally able to get around by myself. I went to get cleared to go back to work, but I failed every physical exam I was given. Why was this happening to me? I felt better, I thought I was doing much better, but I didn't realize that the stroke had done more damage than I knew. My family needed me to provide. After all, I was the head of the house, the man. I had to get back to work. I drifted deeper and deeper into depression. I stopped preaching at my church and turned it over to another preacher. I didn't feel like preaching anymore. I didn't want to go anywhere or do anything. My wife knew something was up with me and she would try to talk to me and be there for me. She would encourage me and tell me that everything would get better. She tried to minister to me with the word. But I wasn't trying to hear what she had to say and eventually, I shut her out completely.

In December, shortly before Christmas, I received a letter from my employer that I had been administratively resigned. I had never heard of such a thing, but later I found out that they could no longer secure my position and because I would not quit and they didn't fire me, they administratively resigned me just to keep me from getting unemployment. When I filed for unemployment benefits, I was denied because they determined that I had quit. The job that I had given more than 10 years of my life to, didn't want to pay me unemployment. That was my breaking point. I remember locking myself in our bathroom. My wife overheard me crying and she began to bang on the door for me to open it, but I wouldn't answer. I had an open pill bottle in my hand, ready to take my life that night. My wife must have called my mother because the next thing I know she was calling me on the phone. She convinced me to unlock the door and I immediately fell in my wife's arms, weeping. I was suicidal and in denial about needing help. Some days, I would drive and sit at a lake, contemplating driving myself and my car in. That wasn't the first time I had suicidal thoughts. Since I was raped these thoughts would often come and go. It wasn't until I got older that I actually attempted to carry them out.

I felt like the only help I could give myself was to kill myself. I didn't care about how it would make anyone else feel. In my mind, I was a poor excuse of a man. On February 14, 2019, I was having a rough day. I wasn't able to do anything for my wife and I felt bad about it. The woman that deserved everything from me was the woman that I had given the least to. But one thing I can say about her, is that no matter what, she has stuck by my side. She's been right there through everything, pushing me to be a better me, even when I didn't want to be. But that night she noticed my speech slurring and I started feeling bad. She immediately rushed me to the hospital. I was told that I couldn't even remember what month it was. I had my second stroke. However, because my wife got me to the hospital in time, the affects weren't as devastating as the first. But mentally, my mind was mess up. I hid it well or at least I thought I did. Even though I wasn't verbally saying anything, my cry for help was present in other ways.

I began to secretly drink and self-medicate, just to ease my pain. While my wife was at work and my children at school, I would sit on my porch and drink, not realizing that the temporary high would only make my depression worse. I continued this cycle for months. Then, right before Mother's Day, I had a heart attack. I watched while the doctors attempted to regulate my blood pressure and slow my heart down. I thought that I was going to die but I thank God that he allowed me to still be here. Even though I was thankful to be alive, I still hadn't dealt with the issues of my mind and once again suicide became an option. I was denied disability, but I couldn't work. My wife was doing everything. I felt like less of a man. My kids were beginning to feel the effects of my issues. Everything was a mess. By the summer of 2019, I had hit rock bottom. It wasn't until my lowest point that I realized I needed some help. What I was dealing with was bigger than the little strength I had. I decided to speak with my physical therapist about what was going on with me. I could no longer live this way. He referred me to a program for those with mental illnesses. I was initially offended. I didn't have a mental illness! I just needed to get myself together. I was not crazy!

Despite my own fears, I decided to begin the program. It was in a group setting with a therapist, kind of like a class. On the first day, I was angry, nervous and wanted to get up and walk out. I didn't know these people and I darn sure wasn't sharing any of my personal business with them. But I knew I wanted to change my life and I knew I needed help, so I stayed. They began to go around the room and share their stories about what brought them to the center. I was like, "Oh, no! This is not for me!" As time progressed, I eventually opened up and talked about situations that I kept bottled up for years. This is when the healing process began. Being a male, especially a black male growing up in the church, there is a stigma about seeing psychiatrists.

We are often taught that mental illness can be cured with the help of God, if you would just allow him to help you through it. And that crazy people are the mentally ill. But having a mental illness does not make you crazy. It does not mean you are unable to function. It does not mean you are a bad person. And seeking help outside of church does not mean you don't have faith in God. With the proper medicine and education, you can get back on track with your life. I believe that God placed psychiatrists here to be able to help us navigate through the tough times. I believe that me getting help for my mental state was God's way of letting me know he had me covered.

Now, my days are happier, I can see the sunshine and my days are not so dark. Now, I can live to face another day. Now, I finally feel like I am truly free. Hopefully, my story will help those who may be suffering from mental illness in silence. I want you to know that a roadblock doesn't have to mean that it's the end of your destiny. I am a living witness that through tragedy, through hurt, through disappointments, through life's struggles, you can live again.

Dominique Marquie Releford has had a passion for acting and writing since he was a young child. Born in Goeppingen, Germany, he was very involved in his church at a young age. Through ministry, he learned to play several instruments and sang in the choir, eventually becoming the praise team leader. As an actor, he has appeared in shows such as Tyler Perry's Ambition, BET's Tales and Saints and Sinners, to name a few. He has also been in various plays and short films, including Second Birthday, Stand Up, and Deliver our Male. Marquie's hobbies include shopping, bowling, and writing songs. He, his wife and their three children reside in Macon, Ga.

CHAPTER 4

THE GAME TAUGHT ME TO FEEL
Brian Walker

Love was not my strongest attribute as a young man. One would think because of the love I had been shown, I would be able to grab the horns of that beast called love and ride it well. Clearly, this was not the case. You see, even though I witnessed what appeared as healthy love, my introduction came with instructions that seemed to be written in Japanese. In fact, assembly was required. I quickly realized that I didn't have the tools. I didn't recognize the importance of reading any of the instructions (they were on the floor over there). How did the product end up looking like the picture on the box (so many pieces)? Who had the glue? I certainly had no idea where to put the batteries.

Listening to the locker room gossip, "CONQUEST" was the word I heard that meant the most to me. I felt the call of the wild and needed to answer. I did choose women that I knew were good for me, but I seemed determined to try my hand at being "slicker than most". You see, the pool of women was vast. My struggles with self-esteem, coupled with my undisciplined life when it came to women, had no bearing on the need for the chase. The game of cat and mouse was exhilarating. With each woman I chose, came another reason to play. Sex was inevitable with most, but I knew how to juggle the bowling pins. If she was new and didn't want to participate in the "naked dance", that was cool. As I dropped her off, I would simply call another that was eager to Rumba, and we danced. There were few times when I didn't have opportunity to improve my numbers.

The trail of confusion, heartache (many were my own), betrayal, lies and even a few angry gazes from brothers, cousins and fathers did not deter me from attempting to reach the pinnacle of my triumphs. Myself, and many of my locker room classmates, failed to understand nor did we care, that we were leaving a trail of disenchanted young girls that would carry with them the memory and experiences of being used and left as casualties of the game. I had no understanding of who I was and the impact upon the ladies that I threw away. I valued nothing but myself and how I appeared to my fellow users, or losers, as it were. FOR THIS, I AM FOREVER REMORSEFUL. I'm a proud father of my own baby girl now and I dare any young man to attempt to manipulate her mind and character, play with her emotions, then snatch her heart from her chest. I am under no disillusion to believe that she will not experience a heartache in her young life, but I'm by her side.

But I continued to stagger from lady to lady, bed to bed, from relationship to failed relationship like a drunken sailor on leave from his battleship. I remained intoxicated with my frivolity and mayhem until I was hit with the reality of that proverbial left hook. You see, there was this woman for whom I had fallen…hook, line, and sinker. She stepped on every one of my emotions. I felt abandoned, mistreated, inadequate, used and lied to. The pain was so intense that it seemed my soul had a hole in it. I could neither eat nor sleep. And the worst part was that no one seemed to care. I was alone with all my thoughts and feelings. It was a very dark time. This was before today's technology. There were no cellphones, Facebook or Twitter, just landlines, pay phones, and answering machines. My imaginations were running wild. Where was she? Who was she with? Was she thinking of me? Was she doing the same things with "him" as she did with me? I was a mess! The ordeal was excruciating. I did get through it, but I was different.

The way I approached life and potential relationships had changed. I was less trusting, less giving, less talkative, less everything. You see, I was still madly in love with the woman, who without care, had thrown my heart over her left shoulder. No matter how much I drank, smoked, slept or worked, I could not shake the memory of her touch, the idea of her love, nor her unforgettable, intoxicating scent of the perfume that launched me into orbit whenever I was lucky enough to fill my nostrils. I was jacked up. That struggle was real. I understand the pain and abandonment felt by the ladies I've left on the discarded path of my destruction. But my greed led me to the chase, even when my hands were full. A bird in hand was not better than two in the bush. I just wanted more. The recurring hurt and pain would last until the next opportunity presented itself, then I would go in again.

The one thing that did change, was the choices I made. I still have the memory of the field of battle, but my uniform is different. No longer am I concerned with the medals pinned to my chest, nor the stripes on my shoulders. But rather, my duty is to respect the space and sanctity of her, appreciate her and to formulate friendships. Quality over quantity, singularity rather than multiples, dignity over degradation. But I took the long road to get here.

Growing up in the Midwest in the 1970s was like living under a veil of protection. So much we didn't know, so much we hadn't heard and so much more that our parents and family members hid from us. We didn't know we were IN THE NEIGHBORHOOD, because everyone else was IN THE NEIGHBORHOOD. We lived amongst each other in peace and harmony for the most part. Minimal crime it seemed, minimal prejudice it seemed... and an overall lovely life that was shielded from the heartaches and mishaps of the cities and states that surrounded us.

Some of my earliest memories were at my grandparents' home on Mill Street in Kansas City, Kansas. I believe it was 1911 N. Mill Street. It was green. I can remember it being a large two-story home with large rooms on a very efficient floor plan. It had a wrap-around porch, a long driveway, and there could have been an alley. It sat on a nice lot with a modest back yard, but it had a dungeon-like crawl space for a basement. My grandmother kept an organized home, but some of the other homes on the street were not as organized. There were families that seemed different than we were, but I had no real gauge to go by. We loved one another the same. Unlike today, financial status didn't seem to matter as much. I was probably six years old. I couldn't have understood. My neighbors became some of the most important people in my life at that time.

I can also remember living in the projects. Gateway was the name. But this was a real multi-family community. It was not the projects. This was our home, the place we lived and loved. We all lived together; it was a village. There were not many fast food joints back then, but there were some neighborhood stores that served food and milkshakes. The barber shops were sterile and professional. At least the one on 5th Street was. Our schools were orderly and efficient. So, we ate, shopped and went to school together. I was a very shy young boy, but I had to trust the village. People helped each other then.

Shaft, Superfly, Dolemite and Bruce Lee were the common figures on the big screen and in our imaginations.

And then there was Pam Grier! We heard angels sing each time she appeared. But I digress. We were discovering our first friends, who were, as we later learned, our cousins, our siblings and our closely-knit neighbors. We played games like hide-and-go-get-it; Simon Says; Red Light, Green Light; Foursquare; and dodgeball. We were at the roller rink to skate every week. The playgrounds were filled with the sound of children bouncing balls, screaming and occasionally fighting. The whistle at recess was both liberating and disappointing. The school lunches were delicious and filling. The sky was fresh and free of pollution. The trees were tall, and the yards were long.

My dad came home from the Army like this mythical figure emerging from the fog. I think it was 1971. I was standing with my mother in our front door. This visual is burned into my recollection. As should be, my father was the most important man I knew. It was a good time for me, when he reentered the family unit.

My dad was a 26-year Army veteran. I believe his rank was Sergeant First Class. He was sharp, disciplined, handsome and huge. Our family dynamic changed. My father had to adjust to civilian life. Although he very rarely spoke of his combat years, he never escaped the images of war. There were demons from the past that occasionally showed up. We dealt with them. He was a strong disciplinarian with an authoritative voice, and even more ominous actions. He was our leader now. We were sometimes afraid, but we were always safe.

My father made strength look easy, but you knew it took fortitude. He loved his family and it seemed he dared anyone to disrespect our unit. He was a hard worker, striving to find his place in society, in his newly realized existence. He had a few jobs he hated, but his family would not suffer, so he went. He loved us the best way he knew how. Over the years, I would recognize his sacrifices, pride and diligence that shaped his life. They are many of the same attributes I carry today, just not nearly as successful. But there was one space, of LOVE, that could only be occupied sufficiently by his first love. That space belonged to my mother.

I can remember my beautiful mother. She is, as the scriptures describes, a weaker vessel (1 Peter 3:7), a vessel deserved of care, compassion, patience, protection and most of all love. She was and still is like expensive stemware fit for fine wine, aged sherry and the most expensive of Champagne.

She consistently wore a well-maintained head of flaming red hair, oftentimes covered by a beautifully designed scarf she would tie under her chin to prevent the wind from damaging its formation. Her face was sprinkled with angel kisses. Her smile would make the devil blush. My mother showed love to everyone but accepted disrespect from no one. She attracted attention everywhere she went but remained grounded and faithful through it all. I used to follow her around my grandparents' home waiting for her to sit so I could lay my head in her lap. Many times, she was hesitant to sit so I would not try to sit too. She would touch me in a way that made me feel loved. She would clean my ears with Q-tips, stroke my hair and sometimes caress my face. She would rock me to sleep in such a gentle way, then wake me with her soothing voice with instructions for me to go to my room when it was time to rest for the night. I was a mama's boy... and still am.

My lockup was in the form of being undisciplined. I was impatient and short on confidence. I lacked realization. I was immature. I didn't understand *me, myself* nor *I*, so I deflected my truth. I had to overcome a speech impediment (stuttering) and I was just plain fearful.

I had wonderful examples of patience, love, freedom, and culture. It took me a long time to understand how they applied to my life. You grow and you learn but we also grow at different paces. Learning is the key. We must be more receptive to learning, accepting and realizing our truths... good or bad.

I was the middle child of three. I have an older brother, whom my father treated a little harsh, and a younger sister, who garnered a lot of love and patience. At times, I felt left out of conversations, opportunities to learn, love and approval. This, of course, was a huge misunderstanding on my part. I was actually viewed as being independent, a free thinker, and a quick learner. In my extreme shyness, I found myself separated from what I really needed. This was probably my first bout with misunderstanding. My father was busy adjusting to civilian life, dealing with his own demons and making a living so that we could have a life. My mother was also adjusting to this new life, tending to my father, working outside of the home, serving at our childhood church, keeping the love and peace at home, trying to save my brother from himself, and raising my sister. At times, I felt alone in a house full of loving people.

I was less of a communicator in my younger years. I found ways not to speak. I should have spoken and cultivated many levels of relationships. But I didn't. There's a boundary to keep, but not so much with the ones you say you love. One should open themselves up to family no matter what. Whatever the hierarchy in your family, talk about, respect and contribute to the betterment of the family. There are a lot of consumers amongst us, but we should each lean toward being a contributor. Discipline yourself for yourself.

As a young adult, my bouts with love were less than savory. As most men believe, love and sex are parallel situations. If we're not having regular porno type sex, we are not loving one another. I had no idea of what real communication between man and woman was supposed to look like. So, I would kick and buck when the "communication" broke down into shouting matches and rounds of silence. It went from one extreme to the other. So, of course, I failed miserably time after time. I married young (the first time). I had no business marrying at 20-21 years of age. I had not traveled outside my cocoon, nor was I mature enough to understand the responsibilities of marriage. It was doomed from the start. I married again and that was no better. She was beautiful, intelligent, driven and articulate. But we were never friends. Please understand that friends will tell each other so much more than husbands and wives. If you are not friends with your lover, you will not be lovers for long!

Along with all this chaos, there were children in the mix. I was not ready, disciplined enough, and nowhere near respectful enough to my children. I was selfish with my communication and my resources and on top of it all, I was absent. There is no excuse for this behavior. One of the most important relationships in this world, is the relationship between parent and child....and I failed. In the ever-ringing words of the great Frederick Douglass, "It is better to build strong children than to repair broken men." My children appear to be thriving in spite of my failure to them and for that I am eternally grateful to my Creator. I love all three equally and pray I can make things right.

Relationships are work; they are never free of conflict. We must understand that not all conflicts are negative conflicts. But I must say, conflicts that do not have an attainable resolve are conflicts unworthy of the time it takes to conjure. Choose your battles and engage in those feverishly, if you must. But don't argue for the sake of arguing, somehow believing it makes for a more concrete union. It does not! So, I had to realize the errors of my ways. I didn't exercise the art of listening. Being a good listener is the key to happiness and longevity. Active listening is listening to understand, not just to respond. Be prepared when traveling down the road of active listening though, because you will hear things you may or may not know. Some things you are not ready to recognize, let alone accept. But you must, especially when the words are true.

I had a hard time speaking to and with people that I didn't know. But how do I get to know you if I do not speak. What a Catch 22! My speech was interrupted around the age of 11 or 12. I'm not sure what happened. My reading began to falter, and my tongue had a mind of its own. I couldn't control the tempo of my words and I was embarrassed. I had the roughest time speaking to my father. As I said before, he was a disciplinarian, a public figure in our city by then with a stern heavy direct voice and he was big. I knew he loved me, but I was nervous each time I had to speak with him, let alone ask for something. He brought it to my attention once, and that's when things began to change. I began to watch the news with great intent. I watched Peter Jennings for the most part and began to understand the art of tempo, emphasis and enunciation. Although I may still struggle from time to time, I now am able to speak to rooms and auditoriums full of people. I've held conversations with vice presidents and presidents of companies, facilitated meetings with decisionmakers, hosted events, performed in stage plays and there is so much more to come. We are all overcomers.

There comes a time when you must accept what is being said. Humility is not deflecting the truth about oneself, but rather, it is accepting the truth. When someone compliments you on something, i.e. a skill, a creation at your hand, your talent or even your appearance, learn to accept it. Show gratitude to the person giving the compliment, thank your Creator and move along without becoming haughty. You see, I didn't quite understand that I was handsome. I didn't realize people thought me to be handsome. I didn't know how to be, act, embrace or reply to the word, nor did I understand what came along with it. So, I deflected the compliments and often thought people to be disingenuous. I have since learned to receive and accept this label. I have been on numerous runways, participated in photo shoots and model competitions. I'm a published model, a contributor to three national magazines and an author.

DON'T EVER QUIT! You can spend money and make more money, but you cannot spend time and make more time. LIVE every day and value those that are in your LOVE. Your **Life**, **Love** and **Lockup** can and will help somebody become more than they were yesterday.

Brian Walker was born and raised in Kansas City, Kansas, and in 1988 moved to Atlanta where he discovered his gift of teaching and bettering the lives of others. After spending time as a driver, he became an instructor in the transportation field. Using driving simulators, computer-based training and real-time driving techniques and practices, Brian traveled the country helping drivers improve decisions behind the wheel. He also turned his love for fitness into becoming a personal fitness instructor. Brian is also an officer for the nonprofit organization "Future Gents", whose mission is to usher young men into the lifestyle of being gentlemen by using the pillars of style, etiquette, manhood, leadership skills, and effective communication.

CHAPTER 5

THE PAIN OF TWO WORLDS
Tobie Famusipe

Being born in the United States and raised in Nigeria has been the biggest culture shock in my life. My whole life I have struggled to balance both worlds and it has affected me in my relationships with friends, family and even my relationships with women that I have dated. Sometimes, it's good; sometimes it's bad. People don't understand my culture, some don't want to understand my culture, and most don't respect my culture.

I come from a highly educated family. Going to college and graduating is law no matter what. The tribe I'm from is Yoruba, a world-renowned culture where we take pride in being educated because that's what our parents, grandparents and great grandparents instilled in us for generations dating back to the colonization days by the British.

Growing up, my siblings and I we were never given the opportunity to express our feelings. Our parents didn't care about how we felt. We were told to do whatever they told us and that was it. We couldn't ask questions so we could learn. The famous response was, "Do as I say, not as I do!"

Being the oldest child had more disadvantages than advantages. I was the one who catered to my other three siblings. I became the parent during my teenage years. I cooked, cleaned and washed clothes for my siblings. I even had to wash and iron my parents' clothing. I never had the chance to really be a teenager. I was forced to be an adult at an early age. As I got older, my parents never allowed me to pursue the things that made me happy. That went for my siblings as well. My parents wanted me to go to school and major in something that *they* wanted me to pursue. The most painful part of it was when they compared us to other children who were doing better than us. It felt like our parents were competing with other parents and their children rather than focusing on our thoughts and feelings. They were also reliving their lives through ours, which is a common thing that most Nigerian families endured and a lot of American Nigerian adults my age can attest to.

If we ever went against anything our parents said or did, we usually got beat up mercilessly, so bad that in America, it's considered child abuse. I wear glasses today because of what my father did to me. My mother was gravely ill and hospitalized when I was 14 and I was responsible for taking care of my siblings. I usually got them ready for school, cooked, cleaned, etc. One morning, I was so tired that I woke up very late. Because I caused everyone to be late, my dad beat me so badly, even kicked me in my right eye. I was bleeding profusely from my right eye and seeing double for weeks. It took my dad over 20 years to apologize for what he did to me.

Parents in Nigeria got away with things like that. And if we didn't get beat up, parents would enforce strange punishments on us such as not eating dinner or lunch or kneeling on both knees with our arms raised and our eyes closed for hours in a corner.

Another strange punishment was called "stoop down", a grueling punishment where you were forced to bend down with one finger touching the ground and raising your right leg up. You couldn't switch legs or fingers or you'd be subjected to even more punishment. It was very inhumane and the most brutal punishment I got when I did something wrong. After hours of 'stoop down', my back would be strained, and

I'd be sweating profusely. I don't believe children should be brought up this way or treated like slaves. Should we do work around the house and help? Absolutely! Should we respect our parents? Absolutely! But to be stripped of not being able to be yourself and be honest felt inhumane. This was part of my pain growing up. I carried this with me for years. I also hated being the oldest child because the traumatic experiences influenced me all the way into my adolescence and adulthood. The mental abuse took a toll on me just as much as the physical abuse. In your mind, you know that parents should love you better than what you are experiencing.

Sometimes, I blame my parents and sometimes I don't, which led me to have a very bitter resentment towards them for many years. Even after I moved back to America, my parents were still trying to find a way to have some sense of control, telling me to start sending money weekly to them once I got a job. It took my uncle and aunt to intervene to help put a stop to the physical and mental abuse I was experiencing. Even as of today, my mother states that it's her right and birthright to still get money from me.

Like I said previously, I blame my parents sometimes and at times I don't. I blame them because I know they had some sense of not doing these horrible things to me and my siblings, especially when they were both educated in the United States. Sometimes, I don't blame them because this is how they were raised. Does that make it right? In my opinion, no because I have witnessed kids who grew up in our culture who did not get the same abuses we got. Those parents made a choice not to abuse their children and found different options to discipline when needed.

Also, part of my pain was the fact that my parents, and Nigerian parents in general, rarely used the word love. Their way of showing love was feeding us and clothing us. No emotional attachments of mom and dad ever existed. I know for a fact that my parents have never told me or my siblings that they loved us. To hear them say they are proud of us when we do something well is like pulling teeth and was a stretch for them. The first time I heard my late father say he was proud of me was when I was in my early 30s. I couldn't believe it. But never did my parents ever say they loved me or my siblings.

Finally, December 1, 1990, when I left Nigeria, it felt like I gained my independence. I missed my siblings, but I didn't miss being with my parents because I had endured so much mental and physical abuse. My mom was notorious for using profane words towards me and my siblings. All the traumatic experiences I had as a kid and adolescence unfortunately followed me to the United States.

After returning to the United States, I felt free, but I was hiding the emotional trauma. I started to live my teenage life in my 20s which didn't make any sense. I had no motivation whatsoever to do anything. I started college and I wasn't serious. I partied instead of focusing on academics. I was getting into trouble with family, smoking weed and doing cocaine, which I used to escape the emotional trauma I endured back home in Lagos, Nigeria.

I realized that my upbringing prevented me from being honest with anyone. I never had the freedom to be myself and was prevented from expressing myself as a child. Every time I was in a relationship, I was afraid to be honest for fear of wrongful judgement and resentment. We were not brought up to be ourselves and express our feelings and thoughts. We were basically shells of ourselves. I still felt like a shell until just a few years ago.

I went from one unstable relationship to another, some of it was my fault because I was afraid to be myself. When I finally met my ex-wife, 19 years ago, I thought I had a breakthrough, but I didn't. I carried the same challenges into my marriage without seeking help or some sort of closure to my traumatic past. I feared being myself in my marriage because my ex was not approachable or receptive to me opening up about my feelings and past experiences, especially when it came to things that would make me happy. I ended up being in a selfish and self-centered marriage which led to me being even more enclosed and not being able to be myself. I did so many things behind closed doors. What my parents did to us was happening all over again. This time, it was with a wife who didn't care about my feelings. As long as I was taking care of her and our daughter, nothing else mattered.

Not being able to be myself hurt me so deeply that I was afraid to ask my ex if I could buy the most simplistic items such as a phone charger or a belt. It was so embarrassing because subconsciously my past was still on my mind and part of the inner demons I was fighting. My ex never paid attention to what was going on with me or even to try to know my past. What made matters worse was when we had our daughter, parts of my upbringing started to manifest itself as we were raising her. I would maliciously yell at her or spank her. I had to catch myself and say, "I don't want to do to my own child what our parents did to us."

Towards the end of my marriage, things were getting worse. It was hard to balance my culture and my upbringing with Nigerian roots (that I'm so proud of) together with my American culture especially when I was with a woman who really didn't care about my family or me. Because of her unwillingness to learn about me as her husband, my culture and my family, it created a gap between us.

The ultimate pain was when I lost my father back in 2014. I withdrew from everything and everybody. I couldn't be myself and became Tobie the imposter, who was in serious pain. I wasn't being honest with my feelings to my ex because she didn't make our environment comfortable for me to really express myself. The demons in me at the time never allowed me to unleash my hurt and pain. My ex didn't care enough to help me through the grieving period of my father's passing. She didn't even encourage me to go home to Nigeria to bury my father. That was the last straw in my marriage.

The Final Battle Against My Pain and the Demons Within

After 46 years of not having a chance to be myself and be honest with myself, I decided (with prayer) to make some moves that were not popular with a lot of people. I did some things in my marriage that I wasn't proud of. It was a final cry for help which my ex completely ignored. There is a saying, "There is a price for freedom", and I was ready to pay it so I could rediscover myself and be free.

I went to counseling twice, once for six months, and once for nine months. I wanted to try to save my marriage and to have a therapist help me in dealing with my pain. My ex never joined me.

After reaching out for help through my therapist and my ex with no response, I decided to file for divorce. Essentially, I got help from my therapist, who assisted me in seeing that my past had been following me my whole life.

After my divorce, I met a beautiful woman whom I'm still with today. I'm so grateful for her in my life, I struggled for a long time to bring my guards down with her, but she never gave up on me, despite the challenges I gave her as I was still hiding within myself. I felt like an onion constantly being peeled by her. I have never in my life met someone who never judged me. Sometimes, I'm scared to express my feelings, but she makes it easier. Even if she doesn't like what I say or do, she appreciates me being me.

After 48 years, and for the first time in my life, I can be free and be myself. I'm with a woman who knows my pain and is helping me through it. And finally, I'm grateful that I've met a woman who genuinely loves me and is not afraid or timid to tell me how much she loves me. For once, I'm not being taken for granted. And it feels good.

Tobie Famusipe was born Babatope Famusipe to Nigerian parents in Washington, D.C. A first generation American-Nigerian, Tobie fell in love with acting at a young age. He loved watching shows and films such as S.W.A.T., The Six Million Dollar Man, and The Cosby Show. After living in Nigeria for 11 years, Tobie learned multiple dialects and accents. He put his love for acting on hold after returning to the United States in 1990 to pursue a college education. After completing college, he landed in the information technology field as an IT business process engineer. In 2013, he returned to his love for acting and has since appeared in more than 40 film and television projects in the Atlanta area.

CHAPTER 6

THEY CAN'T GIVE YOU
WHAT THEY DON'T HAVE
Antonio T. Davis

Thanks for your support
and contributions to Volume 2.

One Saturday morning, the spirit of God reminded me of a lesson long revealed but also long forgotten. I didn't understand it at first revelation, most likely because I hadn't experienced enough "life" to get it completely. So, I guess it was more of a foreshadowing into an understanding that would be revealed at this moment. The lesson explained the part of my life that no matter what I accomplished, I could not seem to satiate. It explained the fact that no matter how hard I tried to please people and become what they wanted me to be to win their love, I always loss. I was locked into a pattern of people pleasing that saw me accomplish all my goals but with a part of me that was never satisfied. After that Saturday morning, things would be different.

Although I had won some superficial victories, I had taken way more losses and some of the losses even disguised themselves as victories. Yes, I graduated from high school, college and graduate school with honors, but what did it really mean? I could regurgitate information, and every now and then actually understand, but still what did it really mean? It meant that I had some paper that signified that I could follow directions well; it means that I conformed to a system…another system. The same means of conforming that saw me fail in other areas of life.

In retrospect, I would say that until my mid-20s, I was a professional conformist. That's all I did. I conformed for my parents, conformed for my school peers, conformed for my jobs and conformed in every manner of relationship in which I had ever been involved. I tried my best to make other people happy while neglecting myself the entire time. I loved to see people happy and still do, but I rarely achieved my desired outcome and in the rare event that I did make someone happy, oftentimes, it was at my own expense. The cost was major. That cost was my happiness and an incredible amount of time that I do not wield the power to get back and the ultimate reward was a combination of heartache, anger, and pain.

My father was born during a time when men were more bread winners than emotionally involved participants in the day-to-day development of the children... outside of being the voice and instrument of discipline. He was born to a father who would set his own house on fire, reasoning that no other man was going to live in that house. My dad recalled losing the school clothes that he had just purchased in preparation for the coming school year. He purchased them on his own with no financial help from his parents. They were not replaced when the insurance money was issued. It was just a loss. Is there any reason that he couldn't put anything different into me? All I ever wanted to do was to please him and my mother. I'm not so sure I ever accomplished it. I remember spending a lot of time and energy being angry about the relationship that I did not have and at times hovering just above a state of depression. All I worked for, all I wanted, was for my father to verbalize his approval of me. The question is this though, how can a man show you value when the man who raised him neither showed him value nor recognized his worth? Can he really give me the things that had not been instilled in him?

Relationships of all sorts have been a source of consistent pain. Yet again, the path to pain was surrounded by my inner desire to be valued and the method of choice was again conforming along with a little bit or more like a wealth of naivety. Sometimes, it was friends or the numerous failed relationships with girls as young boy and women as a man.

Friends can be the greatest assets in the world and at times your biggest liability. My loyalty to them has led me to make some of my biggest mistakes, especially when loyalty came at the cost of self-sacrifice. When I look back, the sacrifice was due to my wanting to feel valuable to someone. It was not about popularity so much as it was the desire for acceptance. In order to gain acceptance, I became what they needed at the moment and at other times what I thought they wanted me to be. I had no idea how inherently self-serving people could be. I thought life would operate like I learned in Bible study, Sunday school and church. Do the right thing for the right reason and life will reward you. The 'do unto others as you would have them do unto you' was how I based everything.

It took my first religion class at Paine College for me to learn how to study for myself. It was after this that I learned that it rains on the just and the unjust alike. So, no matter what I do, both good and bad things will still happen? Then what's the point of it all? I then noticed that people considered me a great guy when they got their way but had little to do with me when they weren't able to manipulate the situation. Saying "no" greatly diminished the circle of friends whom I thought I had and at the same time brought me greater peace. Until then, I hadn't realized how much the words "friend", "family", and "love" were thrown around without recourse. It's sad really. Were they thrown around because of a lack of understanding or few examples of the true practice of these words or was there a gross abuse of these words in order to manipulate a situation for a desired effect? It's hard to say because regardless of the reason, the inappropriate use of the words causes pain wherever they have been thrown around in my life. Either way, I've become comfortable with a smaller circle of influence on one level and increasing my circle on another. My network no longer hinges on emotions but it steadies itself on the foundation of a mutual, beneficial objective.

It seems like church is one of the primary places where my faith has been abused. I would never have to worry about the "people of God" right? Surely everyone who is hearing the same message of love and trust are the same people that I can trust without question. As it turns out, as much as I've heard the messages about doing the right thing, I've also neglected a whole book about wisdom, an entire 31 chapters. One of the biggest betrayals of my faith was that of a man who took me in soon after I walked into this particular church and was quick to throw around the term brother and the popular theme in church around this time, "I love you and there is nothing you can do about it."

Apparently, I remained mentally asleep for the better part of my life. I can't understand how I could have been so naïve. At that time, I was married. My faith was very strong but definitely shrouded in innocence and the same desire to be accepted and loved. It began with a pretty innocent question… "Hey man, can I borrow a few dollars? The government shut down and I'm not getting my check." "Sure," I replied. "I gotcha." I would not be a good Christian if I said no, so I agreed because it was the right thing to do. No! It was the right thing to do, but as it turns out, it was for the wrong person.

This 'brother' of mine would continue to find random reasons why he needed to continue to borrow "a few dollars" at various times. It's because of this incident that I've learned to ask the hard questions and not to ignore signs. As time went on, this married father of two continued to come to me about loans that he never seemed to pay back. I found out he was unemployed, which would explain why he was always available every time the doors of the church were open. When that job topic came up, all of a sudden, he began getting job interviews. I even filled his tank up with gas once so he could get to his interview, which didn't materialize into a job and had him back asking for more "funding". I thought to myself, this guy is either horrible at interviewing or he just has some really bad luck. At least that's what I thought until he said something about buying a dog. A dog? For some reason, this one-minute detail made me inspect his situation with all "Christian" filters off the picture. This 'brother', as I would see, had a wife with a full-time job, two children with mobile phones, a dog, cable, and internet not to mention that he had been running this game with no job the whole time I had attended the church. Dude... I was working as a physical therapy director and teaching at an on-campus university and working at a gym and I didn't have all these things. He had his reasons that justified everything for him but not for me. I didn't just cut him off right there though; I reverted to this rule I had about loans. Now, I haven't been as consistent with this rule as I need to be but more consistent than I had been and hurt a lot less. The next time he showed up to my job with the "pity me, I'm down on my luck face", I had an answer for him. Sure, I can give you the money, but I need you to mow my lawn, clean out my garage or something. Nothing I thought was degrading for any man much less a man who was honestly trying to hold his family down. You would have thought I hurled the biggest insult known to man at him. The way he looked at me was just weird at the time. He was genuinely insulted that I would have the unmitigated gall to ask him to work for the money that he had proven consistent in not paying back. We parted ways that day with my money in my pocket but a bad taste about this man and church people. He pimped me and so did a pastor or two.

It was the first time that I realized that people's perception of anyone's success in life makes them a target. It was then that I realized the cons that go on in the congregation and pulpits of churches. It was also the last time that I was a consistent in my pursuit of God in a brick and mortar church. It hardly seems worth the trouble. I still have my faith, but it is truly now in God and my focus at that point became to put more time into me and far less time and money into other people who have the means to do better. "Life doesn't give us what we deserve. It gives us what we work for." I'm not sure who coined this phrase, but if you're not willing to work for it, I'm not willing to work for it for you. I see that I can't care more about your situation than you do.

When it comes to pain, nothing hurts more than my failed relationships with women. I've spent my time loving people in a manner that I thought was the right way. I conformed to what society deemed as the proper way a man should love a woman, but it turns out that advice was wrong. I loved my wife, who has long since become my ex-wife, the wrong way. I loved the mother of my children the wrong way. I loved my most recent girlfriend the wrong way. As of this moment, I have no idea if we're on pause or over. When

I look over the course of all my relationships, I've loved everyone the wrong way. But my relationships with women have led to some of the darkest moments of my life. I've been so depressed that the only reason that I got out of bed was the routine of going to work and serving people that actually paid for the help and conversations. It was in these moments that having a job as opposed to my being an entrepreneur was honestly one of the things that saved me from my depression. The people whom I served physically were serving me emotionally.

Honestly, I have witnessed very few successful relationships and when I hear about people who have been married for 20 years or more, it just seems strange. How did that happen? How did you make it that long? I've never had a relationship last over three years that I can remember. My marriage only lasted 16 months…a long 16 months. I've seen more examples of failed marriage than successful ones which makes me wonder if the 50% divorce rate is understated. Even the marriages that make it for extended periods don't seem to give me the utopia that marriage is sold on.

My first break up was not the hardest. They all hurt the same to me. When I lock into a relationship, I'm all the way in. Reckless abandon may be great in testosterone-driven sports, but maybe not so much in relationships. I've never committed to any relationship half-heartedly. I entered every one of them with reckless abandon. Surely, if I love her with all that I have and do the right thing, it'll all return back to me. The problem was the same mouth I've used to lavish words of praise on a woman is the same mouth that also hurls the harmful words to the same woman I love. It was my reckless abandon. I lived for the highs of the relationships, but the lows left me fiending like a drug-starved addict. As much as I considered myself an adult, I acted like one of the toddlers that I teach when I didn't get my way. Not everything set me off though. The primary thing on which it all rested was not getting the love that I depended on a relationship to provide. Because so much of my happiness rested on them, I responded in what looked like anger but in actuality was a deep hurt from the same wound that has been reopened either every time I failed to receive love or when a relationship is terminated with the pain of a dagger to the that very same wound.

I realized when I looked at the women I've dated, most of them had the same factors that I had in my life...no honest and good examples of what a good relationship was. Sure, some of them had examples of long-lasting relationships but very few. Even with those few, they were examples of people who only spent time with each other when they went to bed but avoided each other all day. Some had examples of domineering mothers, whom they followed and failed to realize they would end up single or committed to a loveless cohabitation of sorts, just like their mothers. I wanted more than this, so I figured if I could become what they wanted me to be, then we would be happy. I failed. I've failed so many times that I can't help but wonder if love is just an ideological construct that is unattainable. I love God most certainly, but the touch of a woman is tangible and therefore the realest expression of love to me. Can it really be found with anyone?

On this particular Saturday morning, the spirit of God reminded me of a lesson. On this day, as I reflected on life and my experiences since then, the spirit of God made it all clear. With the exception of a few outliers, no one caused me pain intentionally. They could only give me what they had and nothing more. My father, my real friends, my family and my exes... The more I learned to love and value myself, the less often I've experienced pain and the better I could love others. I'm a long way from perfecting this self-love but I've traveled a long road from my self-loveless beginnings. On that Saturday, I realized that I was most successful when I was who God called me to be. I'm quirky. I'm ambitious. I'm driven. I'm reckless. I'm passionate. I see things other people don't. I don't see things other people do. I don't like when people don't use a possessive pronoun before a gerund. I love me. I accept me. I'm okay with being me. I love my father. I love my mother, of course. I love my children. I love all the women who attempted to love me the best way they could, and I apologize for the pain that I've caused you. I love everyone that went into teaching me how to love me and to grow so that my possibilities are endless. After that particular Saturday morning, things became different. Thank God for His infinite wisdom in helping me to understand that everyone who touched my life gave me everything they had to give.

Antonio T. Davis is a multi-talented go-getter who keeps himself busy as a singer, songwriter, event host, physical therapist, mentor, and coach. TraMel, as he is called, is a native of Conyers, Georgia, and prides himself on being the ultimate gentleman. As director of physical therapy, TraMel, extends his passion for sharing health and wellness with others. A graduate of Paine College, who also earned a master's degree in physical therapy from Medical College of Georgia, he is a huge proponent of education being a vehicle for achieving success. As a result, he's incorporated teaching into every facet of his life. TraMel is also a proud member of Omega Psi Phi and is a proud father.

MICHELLE S. LOVETT

CHAPTER 7

LET THE CHANGE HAPPEN
Anthony Velvet Hall

We have all heard the familiar saying: "Life is a journey". It's a convenient summary of our time on this planet. Simply put, a journey is commonly defined as the act of going from one place to another. Such a simple definition could be interpreted as the act itself being simple. Nothing could be further from the truth. Throughout the pages of this book, my brothers have shared with you those two things: a part of their journey and the truth they discovered in it.

Having said that, I'd like to share a part of mine with you. I was in the gym one day and saw a familiar face. She was someone I went to high school with. We'd been in this gym several times but never seemed to cross paths. I wanted to speak to her but was too shy (imagine that!). As I left the gym after my workout, she happened to be on the elliptical machine positioned directly in front of me. She looked at me, smiled and waved. I waved back. I didn't stop and talk to her, but I eventually would. I'd been lifting heavy weights for an hour prior to leaving. Now, I was trying to get through the door blushing while carrying a smile that felt like it weighed a ton.

I'd see her at the gym and got to know her. Those conversations laid the groundwork for a relationship with this wonderful woman. She was everything I wanted in someone... beautiful, statuesque, and driven. Her looks had me captivated but her ambition and fearlessness were qualities I secretly admired. More importantly, we leaned on each other not because of anything bad, but because we both wanted the other to be better. Our relationship prospered despite some trying times. We got through those challenges unscathed and better than before. No matter what my past consisted of her, I looked at her and saw my future. All seemed well until a fateful January day in 2013.

I'd just gotten off work and was making plans to be with her for the evening. I'd made it home when I got a phone call from one of her family members. I was told over the phone that she was on a treadmill at the gym and went into cardiac arrest as a result of a pre-existing heart condition. In an instant, my entire world stopped. At that moment, nothing was more important. I drove my car frantically to the emergency room just hoping to see her. I went in and she was incapacitated. My heart sunk in a flash. She was hanging on by a thread but still alive.

Time has a strange way of standing still when every second counts. Seconds turned into minutes. Minutes turned into hours and hours turned into days. Her condition varied from one day to the next. Then, I'd gotten the news that gutted me. Due to her condition, there was nothing the doctors could do for her. My entire world came crashing down around me. My life was about to change in an instant. Four days later, she passed away peacefully. My baby was gone.

When a loved one unexpectedly passes away, our natural defenses weaken or completely disappear. I was hurt, lonely, confused, and angry, all at the same time. Being in such a state made me vulnerable. When your defenses are down, it's an invitation for the wrong people to enter your life. I learned this lesson three days after we laid my girlfriend to rest. A co-worker began emailing me at work under the guise of concern shrouded in religion. Matthew 7:15 states, "Beware of false prophets who come to you in sheep's clothing, but inwardly are ravening wolves." This wolf had a hunger not only for me, but other men as well. This dalliance didn't last long. Wolves need the same things we all need: love, shelter, and food. But if I learned one thing about wolves after that situation, I learned it's not the hungry ones you've got to watch out for; it's the thirsty ones!

When that situation ended, I reconnected with an old friend from high school. She and I had long talks about our childhood and high school days. That friendship would morph into a relationship. Things went well for a while until a few of our mutual friends tried to involve themselves in our situation. I have never been in a situation where our every move was watched and monitored by people outside of the relationship. I don't think the mutual friends wanted us to fail. I think they just wanted to be a part of the situation themselves. Because my new girlfriend had her own personal problems, I couldn't be there for her like I should have because I was still trying to heal myself. As a result, I ended the relationship after a year. Our breakup wasn't bitter as we are still very good friends to this day.

After my four-year relationship with my angel ended unexpectedly, I'd already been in a brief situation and a year-long relationship with two other women. This pales in comparison with the crazy amounts of emails and inboxes I got from women immediately after my situation ended. I had one female friend who I thought was perfect in every way. She and I got to be a lot more than friends. Indirectly, she hinted at a relationship, but I declined it. It was not easy to do. Because I was rebuilding myself, I didn't want to put myself in a similar situation as before. We remain very good friends to this day.

The isolation did me well as I slowly started to find myself again. It was at this time that I had to take time to accept what had happened. I took away from everybody and dealt with it. Emotionally, I had hit rock bottom. I had lost all my emotional strength and needed to rebuild. So how did I do it? Solitude.

I needed time to rebuild myself for myself by myself. I did this in the most unconventional way you could think of. I allowed myself to become uncomfortable. My life up to that point had been very stable. I had a good job and an associate's degree. My girlfriend and I always encouraged each other. We always talked about the future. I was less than 15 credit hours away from receiving my bachelor's degree when she passed. She was always encouraging me to keep going even when my studies got the best of me. However, losing her made me realize that tomorrow is not promised to any of us. We are all guilty of letting great opportunities pass us by. There are many reasons for this. We may not want to disrupt the comfort in our lives. We may like the way things are. We may fear the change that comes with trying something different, even if it changes things for the better.

It was at that moment that I decided that when the day came that my earthly tabernacle would dissolve, I would go to my grave with memories and not regrets. I had thought about doing some acting but did not want to risk my current standing at my job. After a while, I began taking chances thanks to having built up so many vacation days at work. My first experience was extras work on the BET television series *The Game*. I got on set and really came out of my shell. I did what directors asked of me but was still in awe that I was on an actual television set. It was amazing! I started to really get into acting. I took a few more bookings and got to see myself on television a bit more. It was therapeutic for me. I began to find myself again slowly but surely. A few years after, I met someone who would change my life forever.

I met Troy Bland through a mutual friend. He is an accomplished actor and has performed in various film, television, and theater productions. Troy connected me with C. Nathaniel Brown, better known as Chuck, who was filming a romantic comedy called *55 Seconds* and asked me to be in it. I jumped at the chance. This was going to be my very first speaking role in any production. I didn't have very many lines but I had plenty of fun. I learned a lot as well and made some new friends on set. That one movie jump-started a career that I'm still deeply immersed in today.

By my own admission, I am relentless when pursuing something that I truly want. Acting helped me find myself again. As a result, I wanted to be as good at it as I possibly could. I started reading books and going to seminars that were acting related. All the while, I was applying for more acting roles. I'd seen so many people in roles get typecast. I wanted to become a versatile actor. I began to land more roles and go to different auditions. On the Investigation Discovery show *Murder Chose Me,* I played the role of a cold-blooded killer. On the flip side, I played an emasculated husband in the feature film *Fixation 2.* Two different roles that fell on opposite sides of the character spectrum. Casting me has not always been easy for directors. As a former professional wrestler, my physical proportions are above average. Still I have always tried to get the best out of my performances, no matter what role I have been cast for.

Six years ago, I had absolutely no idea where my life was headed. I'd lost the best thing that ever happened to me and had no clue what tomorrow would bring. Today, I am an accomplished actor and author with nearly 15 film, television, and new media credits to my name (and counting). On top of that, I graduated with a bachelor's degree from DeVry University. Things in my life have changed because of change. Some change was welcomed but most of it was not. The thing about change is that it WILL happen in your life whether you are ready for it or not. Change is the brutal reminder that no matter how in control we think we are, we really are not. All change is not bad. Change is like hitting the reset button on life. All that remains after change has occurred is the same that has always been there: opportunity. It is what you do with that opportunity that determines what happens next.

Since my changes have occurred, I've had people who encountered their own personal storms share their stories with me. I had a classmate lose her significant other not too long after I'd lost mine. I had a co-worker who had gotten divorced after a long marriage. They both had to deal with change. After the change, they asked the question most people ask when change happens: Now what? My advice to anyone whose life is immediately changed by change is simple... Let the change happen! Change can leave you so hurt and confused that you will try to feel with your brain and think with your heart (no, that is not a misprint). You may be tempted to seek refuge in a stranger who poses as a friend. Be careful. Remember my earlier statements about wolves?

Changes like these can help you to truly discover yourself because that is where your answers lie... within. Being hurt and confused is a dangerous combination that not everyone can recover from. Your defenses are down. Your soul is weary. You don't always make the best choices. In fact, the potential to make bad choices will never be greater. Sometimes, people turn to their vices to help them deal with these changes or to avoid thinking about them altogether. Know that when you feel your weakest, you must look inside yourself to find where your strength truly lies. When you come to the realization that what you seek is not in front of you or around you, searching within yourself becomes so much easier. No matter what you are going through, keep going. There is so much greater waiting for you on the other side.

Peace and love, y'all.

Anthony Velvet Hall is a former professional wrestler turned actor. He has appeared in nearly 15 film, television, and new media productions. You may have seen him in such productions as Murder Chose Me, Fixation 2: Uprising, and the TV One television series Fatal Attraction to name a few. Anthony studied at both Georgia Military College and DeVry University, graduating with an Associate of Science in General Studies and a Bachelor of Science in Technical Management – Sales and Marketing, respectively. A native of Newark, NJ, Anthony has been living in Milledgeville, GA, for over two decades.

MICHELLE S. LOVETT

Thank you Teyuna for your loving support!!! author [signature]

CHAPTER 8

FAITHFULLY DRIVEN
James Thornton

When I reflect over my life, I realize how my blessings came at a hefty cost and my brokenness is what built my character. I have suffered throughout my life and experienced varying degrees of pain that included the divorce of my parents, the abandonment by my father, the deaths of people close to me and so many others that I tried to understand along the way.

I was a year old when my father divorced my mother. They experienced some difficult times, from what I was told. People that knew them always said, "They still loved you." My mom did the best she could raising me in Albany, Georgia. But I didn't know my dad. There were so many questions I wanted answers to, but they remained unanswered. As a kid, the thing that hurt me the most was that my father lived four blocks from me and did not make any attempt to see me. He didn't reach out or want to take me places. I felt the abandonment and blamed his actions on his denial that I was his son.

My mother would always say my father was no good. As a young child, I had no understanding of how a father would not be there for his own child. I had school events and performances, including the band, and I wished my dad could have been there to support me. Reflecting on this story is painful but every time I thought about the pain I felt, it taught me to be a better person than he was. What kind of man could live four blocks from his child but never make any attempt to call or visit? Talk about pain and agony! I used to feel as if I was standing in front of an oncoming semi-truck expecting to be saved just before impact...only to be hit over and over again.

As a teenager, I used to hear, "You look just like your father!" My response was, "How can I look like someone I don't know?" It was a weight that I did not deserve to carry but I had no choice. The burden was heavy every time I thought about the stories of my dad.

My mother went into labor with me in the home where they were living. She almost died from hemorrhaging in the bathtub because no one wanted to get her to the hospital. It was a lot of chaos back then, so I was told. I always asked myself what kind of man would allow his wife to go through an ordeal of this magnitude, and allow his family to treat his wife in a degrading manner? Well, he did. I can't say it was intentional, but I felt like things could have been better. Back then, there was no counseling and most of our families relied on home remedies. Mental illness was an issue that needed to be addressed also.

There was no communication between my dad and me. When I asked my mother about my father, she would get extremely upset with me. I was not supposed to come in this world, but almighty God had preordained plans. There are a lot of young boys looking and wondering where their fathers are, or looking for someone to be a father figure and mentor them. The hurt and pain followed me wherever I went because I was wondering and searching all my life. The people who loved me couldn't understand the pain that I was feeling.

Having his last name was one of the things that I despised. Because of the hatred I developed in my heart for him, I wanted to change my name. I remember saying to God, "Lord, no matter what happens, I will never depart from my wife and kids. They will remember the good times and bad. They will know that I love them."

The bible talks about fathers abandoning their children. 1 Tim 5:8 says, "But if anyone does not provide for his own and especially for those of his household, he has denied the faith and is worse than an unbeliever." My father failed to obey God's command. He was paying child support, but that could never replace the quality time that was missing. Sometimes, I didn't even realize the amount of pain and anger I had because my father wasn't there.

I remember one time knocking on his door and asking to see him, but his family told me no. I never knocked again. I was eight years of age at the time. Throughout my teenage years, I always wanted to get to know him. Not only was I missing my father in the natural, I feel like there was also a spiritual abandonment or I was somehow spiritually isolated.

I was angry at people for seemingly no reason. Anything that went wrong, I blamed others, but it would always come back to me. But because of all the pain and mental suffering, I chose to ignore it and it almost cost me the one true person that I loved the most...my wife. During those years of my frustration, she stayed silent. There was anger, resentment, pride, selfishness, and conceitedness. I could not see past myself. I was afraid to grow as a husband, and a father. There was a lot of work that needed to take place in me, but I knew that I had to deal with my issues if this pain would eventually become my character.

I finally met my father. I was 20 years old, and he was 48 and lying in his casket. He died of cirrhosis of the liver. He was an alcoholic and I had no idea I would be following in his footsteps. Due to the nature of his death, I began to see that he had issues. His father wasn't there for him, either. When I attended his funeral, his immediate family acted as if I didn't exist. This added to the thorn in my flesh.

For so long, I felt the whole world was against me. When I thought of a good relationship, I envisioned stability. I needed balance because there wasn't any in my life. I just wanted a relationship that I thought I could handle despite the abandonment.

The things that occurred when I was young was a test. Just like Job in the bible I had to endure. I didn't blame God for the things happening in my life. There was a reason I didn't commit suicide at an early age. I understand there was purpose in everything thing. The issues that consumed me aren't as significant today. I fought mentally every day through good times and bad times to win.

In 1994, I join the U.S. Navy, trying to mask all the pain from verbal abuse. Over the course of my career, I watched other service members deal with their pain, but I could never get a hold of mine. When people would say the wrong things to me, I would snap and act like it was normal. There was a chief petty officer whom I didn't care for who always yelled at me, especially when I yelled at someone else. I remember I was on duty and there was a domestic violence case. I was the watch commander for the shift. The command duty officer was asking me questions about another chief who had assaulted his wife. To shorten the story, I attempted to contact everyone but did not contact NCIS. The next morning, my lieutenant told me good job, but my Chief didn't seem to agree. He called me into his office and told me that I should have informed him of what happened. When I tried to explain to him that I called and left voice messages, the conversation became one sided. He cursed me out, verbally degraded me and disrespected me as a man. At that point, I was so angry that tears rolled down my face. At 34 years old, I should not have had to endure the disregard or disrespect. I hated him for a while, not recognizing I was only holding myself back by giving so much of my energy to someone who did not deserve it.

There was a time when we were deployed, he suffered from gallstones. But the hatred I had for him only made me feel worse instead of better. As I was transferring, I didn't talk with him because he taught me a valuable lesson and that was never be evil and cause others pain... as he did. The situation taught me to be a better sailor. But my mask was still covering my face. Things got even worse when I came from Afghanistan in 2009. My first night at home, I was drinking and later in the evening as I went to sleep, I was having nightmares trying to cope with the fact that my father wasn't around to talk to. It was becoming the norm and I was trying very hard not to be like him, yet apparently looking more and more like him every day.

The year 2011 was a mix of good and bad. It was the year our youngest child was born, and the same year my mother died. I did not know at the time what her condition was and how serious it had become. But like many of us, we always feel that our parents should live a long time, especially mom. There was a time in my life where my mother and I did not see eye-to-eye. She would always say things like everything you do reminds me of your father. When I was 21, my mother took out a warrant for my arrest for criminal trespassing, and yet I still loved her.

After our son was born in August 2011, my wife and I traveled back to Naples, Italy, from Germany. A few months later, I got a message through Facebook from my cousin saying that I needed to call my mom's sister. The news was not good. My wife and I flew back to the states from Italy so I could be with my mom during her last days on earth. There was a lot of selfishness from me. I wanted my mother to live a lot longer. I asked the doctor what was wrong and then doctor informed me that my mom was dying from congested heart failure. It was something that I had never heard of. My brother and I sat by her bedside at the hospital watching her go in and out of her sleep. The conversation that I had with the doctor was not a pleasant one.

Another feeling I had was that my mother could be saved even if she had gone into cardiac arrest. Well, that didn't happen, and God is the only one that could have saved her. But I did not realize it at the time. It wasn't my decision for her to leave me and my brothers. After my mother was transported to hospice, my brother stayed with her until she passed away. He called me and gave me the news. I got up and drove to the hospice. When I saw my mom, the look on her face was priceless. There was a smile and it was the look of peace. I was saddened she was gone and as the oldest son, I became even more lost and devastated because I could not pick up the phone and call her. That was enough pain to last a lifetime.

I was a broken man in so many ways. I was still trying to understand my parents' relationship, the abandonment issues and the loss of my mother, while hoping to get through a deployment without hurting a higher-ranking officer.

Later, I relived some of the conversations I had with my mother, trying to understand some of the things she would say to me about my dad. She loved him even when he walked out on us. In today's African American culture, there are a lot of broken homes where male and female have disagreements, or they can't get along and all it does is affect the kids.

The more pain I felt, the more I tried to drown my pain by drinking alcohol which didn't help. All the covers were pulled over my head. Three things that helped me get through those tough times:

- I told myself that I can't go on living like this if I am going to continue to stay married.
- I have children (3 boys) who are dear to both my wife and me.
- Counseling really helps me.

The drinking stopped four years ago this September. All I ever wanted to do was become the best father, husband, mentor for my wife and children. My whole life was one big circus. The reason those things occurred the way they did and kept lingering over my head is because I had never had the chance to tell my father I forgave him for not being there. The bible says forgive us for our trespasses as we forgive those who trespass against us. I always thought forgiveness was a process, but it is a decision that had to be made. Lately, the word forgive has plagued my mind. The lesson here for me was that even though times were rough emotionally, there needed to be a spiritual renovation. Because of that, God brought me out of a bondage that tormented me for so many years. God took me from Albany, Georgia, to travel all the way to Sigonella, Sicily, where I met my queen.

Even though I was broken, I stayed humble. A good pastor talked about brokenness. It is so precious in the eyes of God. There has to be a spirit of brokenness in our worship to God. We struggle with our own attention as men. It is our strength that draws God's attention. God responds to brokenness. But he does not rush in and save the day like Superman. 1 Sam 16:7 says, *"But the Lord said to Samuel, 'Do not look at his appearance or at the physical stature, because I have refused him. For God does not see as man sees; for man looks at the outward appearance but God looks at the heart.'"*

God knew my desires and the things that were happening. He knew that it wasn't strength or stature that he required but willingness, just like David. Brokenness makes room for God to release his strength through our weakness to accomplish his plans. After David went through his ordeal, he had to humble himself. Psalms 51:16 says, *"For you do not desire sacrifice, or else I would give it. You do not delight in in burnt offering."* It means a ritual without repentance is useless. However, with the right heart and attitude, sacrifices were acceptable. Just know, men, because I've had brokenness, I am humble and when you have brokenness along with humbleness, God will exalt you. So, sometimes it's the strongest people who hide the deepest pain. There is nothing weak about being real with ourselves. We will never get the things in life until we face what is causing our pain. Once I let go of the things that were hindering and tormenting me, including the verbal abuse and abandonment, I let go and let God take control. Trust me when I say this... all I went through was difficult, but I made it through. Remember, great things happen when you let go of the things that weigh you down and your pain can reveal everything that is good about you.

James E. Thornton was born and raised in Albany, Georgia. A graduate of Columbia College with degrees in General Studies, Sociology and Criminal Justice, James is a highly decorated retired United States Navy War Veteran. He has devoted more than 20 years of his life to selfless military service and after retirement continues to serve in his community. He had been deployed to multiple wars and witnessed some devastating events. During his years of service, he has traveled the world and lived abroad for more than 14 years. He and his wife reside in Atlanta.

CHAPTER 9

A TRIP TO JOB'S HOUSE
Bennie Lovett

In January 1963, a United States Air Force Recruiter visited Sylvester, Georgia. He explained to Bennie Nicholas, my best friend, and I the benefits of joining the United States Air Force. I asked the recruiter, "When do I sign up?" He said, "You will have to pass the test in Jacksonville, Florida." I replied, "I can pass the test." My friend and I left immediately on our trip to Jacksonville, Florida.

After passing the entrance examination, I was shipped to Lackland Air Force Base in San Antonio, Texas. After basic training, I was assigned to Altus Air Force Base in Oklahoma. From Altus, Oklahoma, I was shipped to South East Asia. This was during the time that our country was involved in the Vietnam War. Like many others, I was exposed to the deadly, Agent Orange. Following this tour of duty, I was shipped to Homestead, Florida, where I met the love of my life, Gloria D. Sumler. We were married and formed our blended family. This is when God blessed us to raise six children: Gloria, Emmanuel, Tommy, Jacqueline, Donna and Michelle. I was assigned to Homestead Air Force Base for nine consecutive years. This, too, was a wonderful blessing for us. God, our combined salaries, and faithful humble beginnings assisted us allowing us to acquire different investments, real estate, and a different type of living arrangement, from which we both were accustomed. The best part was we both knew all our help came from the Lord.

In 1977, I received orders and was assigned to Incirlik, Turkey. This was a 15-month tour, unaccompanied, which meant that my family would not be moving with me to Turkey. During this time, the Lord blessed us with another addition to our family, a baby girl, Michelle S. Lovett. We were so excited. Michelle was born prematurely on my birthday (September 7). She weighed less than four pounds with complications of her lungs and heart. I asked the Air Force to give me a deferment so that I could remain with my wife and critically ill newborn daughter. However, my deferment was denied. This was a great disappointment to me. I felt like I was letting my family down, even though everything was out of my control.

However, I honored my assignment and was shipped to Turkey. This was one of my most difficult assignments. Everything weighed heavy upon my heart. Michelle was our first biological child together. My being shipped away, leaving my wife with our baby being critically ill, was overwhelming. A few days after she was born, the doctors called the family and told us to come to the hospital. Michelle was not expected to live. She suffered with a heart murmur and issues from being delivered prematurely. Doctors said research and statistics show most babies that encountered both cases don't survive. However, God performed a miracle and turned that situation around in our favor. So, now at the age of 43, Michelle, our baby daughter of the family, is doing amazing things with her life. I'm sure you have read about her, seen her in one of the many plays she has participated in, social media or seen her on TV.

I retired from the Air Force in November 1985 having served actively 23 years and 11 months with two tours in Vietnam. I started working as Chief Code Enforcer for Florida City, becoming extremely active in both the church and community. Time caught up with me again in 2006. I was diagnosed with prostate cancer, yet another disappointment. I took an imaginary trip to the house of Job, by reading the Old Testament book of the Bible. I asked Job, "What do I do? How do I get through this?" I imagined that Job said, "This is easy Bennie. I lost everything I had, including my health. Yet, I never lost my faith that God would bring me through this trouble. So, keep the faith and stay close to God." I'm so thankful my parents brought me up as a believer.

God did it again. He spared my life and the cancer went into remission. I took the holistic approach for healing (seed transplant). That process was new at the time. However, prayer, supplication, and faith led me that way. NO ONE KNEW WHAT I WAS GOING THROUGH BECAUSE I DIDN'T LOOK LIKE WHAT I HAD BEEN THROUGH. I returned to work and lived normally.

When my parents died, the pain was excruciating, even though they both lived to see their 80s and 90s. I realize no matter the age, losing parents, spouses, children or siblings is truly a different pain. Well in 2009, I was faced with the kind of pain that's indescribable. No band aid could cover this wound. I didn't think I would ever recover. THE LOVE OF MY LIFE, MY BESTFRIEND, MY WORLD, MY WIFE OF 40 YEARS, GLORIA LOVETT, DIED. Gloria was sick off and on but honestly, I didn't know she was going to die. She was so strong and independent, even through her most trying time. We had gone to our granddaughter's wedding in Georgia. Later that night, Gloria mentioned that she wasn't feeling well. The next day, I told her we could just return home (to Florida). However, she insisted we go to Michelle's house in Atlanta. Everyone knows when the Queen speaks, her King grants her command. We arrived at Michelle's house and Gloria kept saying how blessed we were and thanking God for all he had done. The next morning, she told us she was ready to go to the nearest hospital. She was admitted to the hospital, but still I just knew things would turn around. I will never forget standing there looking at Gloria when she quickly uttered, "Bennie, Bennie, I'm so sick!" As she called my name, she fell into a coma while I stood over her bed. I felt helpless as I stood there with the medical staff. Gloria slipped away to heaven. I didn't know what I was going to do. How would my children, family and friends receive the news?

Losing my wife caused me to slip into a deep hole of depression, not knowing if I could ever recover. Then I took another imaginary trip to Job's house. Again, Job said, "Remember, Bennie, I lost my children, my wealth and my health. But God gave it all back to me two times more than what I had. Bennie, you can make it…keep the faith and always trust God." I was broken but not destroyed. Three months later, Michelle called and said, "Dad, the doctor informed me today that I must have a total hysterectomy." My child needed her mom more than ever. We prayed and in May 2010, Michelle had surgery. I did my best to help her, but I was still mourning. Thank God for our oldest daughter Gloria, who came and assisted us both. We all realized we needed God and each other.

Shortly after I began to come around, I received another painful stab. The pain couldn't be suppressed. On Veteran's Day (November 11) 2010, I received a call from Tampa, Florida, that my only biological son, Tommy Lee Lovett, was dead. He had endured many hardships in his life. After being shot in a senseless shooting while serving in the Army at Fort Riley, Kansas, Tommy was paralyzed from the waist down. Yet, he pursued and earned his bachelor's degree from the University of Houston. Tommy was a celebrated real estate broker and authored a book titled, *Doors Wired Shut*. The book illustrated the truth about discrimination and disabled veterans. He left behind his beautiful intelligent daughter, Tiffany Terrell, whom I am well pleased with and extremely proud of.

With so much chaos in my life at the time, I had to seek mental and emotional help from a psychologist, physical help from my medical doctor, and spiritual guidance from my Father God and Christ Jesus.

Things began to get better in my life. Yet, on Thursday, October 25, 2018, another heartbreak and disappointment occurred. My daughter, Donna Lovett Maldonaldo, went home to be with the Lord. Donna was a beautiful young lady, very active at Homestead Senior High School, the first captain of the dance and flag line at the home of the Broncos. Donna never met a stranger. Her death required another trip to Job's house, a knock at midnight.

On November 12, 2011, I was blessed to get remarried to Onetha Gillard-Lovett. I'm thankful for our marriage. We both are on our second marriage and our first spouses preceded us in death.

In October 2019, 14 years after my prostate cancer went into remission, disappointment returned. The cancer was no longer in remission and my visit to Job's house solidified my faith in the words and promises of God that He will sustain me. I will conclude by saying... I can't give up now. I've come too far from where I started from. Nobody told me my road would be easy. However, I don't believe God would bring me this far just to leave me. Plus, I still got work to do.

Thank you, baby girl, for sharing your platform with me and others.

Bennie Lee Lovett grew up on a farm in Sylvester, Ga., the sixth of eight children to James and Maggie Greene Lovett. He learned business and work ethic from his father who taught him to work around the farm, including planting seeds, harvesting, and driving trucks of fruit and produce. He excelled in and out of school, quickly learning bricklaying, plumbing, electrical, carpentry, and painting. A Vietnam veteran, Bennie would go on to run several successful businesses, including a limousine service and real estate, and become commissioner of Florida City, Florida.

MICHELLE S. LOVETT

100

ABOUT THE CURATOR

Michelle S. Lovett is the visionary behind Life, Love & Lockup. She was born on September 7, 1976, at Homestead Air Force Hospital in Homestead, Florida, to Bennie and Gloria Lovett, (Deceased). She was born premature with a heart murmur, severe allergies and battling chronic asthma. She had to fight to live. Doctors declared death at birth.

Life circumstances haven't been able to deter her from pursuing her dreams of becoming an A-list actor, author, entrepreneur or giving back in the process. Since the age of 4, Michelle has been able to remember and recite extended material in church and school productions. People always told her she was extremely talented and gifted, but that gift was put on the back burner for years.

The Miami native, youngest of six children in a blended family, spent a lot of her youth in church watching her parents serve. She followed their footsteps, serving on the usher board, singing in the choir and participating in holiday productions. It was also through her parents' examples that she excelled in school, became active in the community, was inducted into the National Honor Society (College) and gifted programs, and held several leadership positions.

Upon graduating high school, Michelle enrolled at Paine College. The transition was challenging and she became unfocused, leading her to Georgia Military College where she earned an Associate's degree in Criminal Investigations. Later, she enrolled at Albany State University completing all courses in Criminal Justice. One of her dreams was to become a judge so she could positively impact the community. Later, she earned a Bachelor's degree in criminal justice from Strayer University.

Michelle spent 10 years working in the financial industry, climbing the ranks and holding leadership roles as conversion specialist, manager and fraud investigator. Michelle's entrepreneurial mindset soon re-emerged. She watched her parents run several successful businesses. Michelle combines her learning and corporate managerial skills from the bank in 2012 and opened MEME'ENT, an entertainment company, managing independent artists, and promoting events. In late 2014, she opened and operated TEAMUP TRUCKS, a trucking company.

Michelle re-evaluated life and what she wanted from it. She walked away from the corporate world, slowed operations on the trucking company, and found a special joy working in the entertainment industry. In 2015, Sista Girl London offered her a role in her stage play and she returned to acting. In 2016 and 2017, she struggled and battled with lupus. Doctors gave her six months to live. She was forced to stop acting. But Michelle started a new regiment and began living a holistic lifestyle.

Two years passed and God proved once again that Michelle is his child. She was alive, healthy and death wasn't in the forecast. She returned to the stage, television, and film, gaining acting experience and quickly becoming a sought-after actor in the Atlanta area. She has done background work for television shows such as Black Lightning; Cobra Kai;

BET Cancer Survivors; Tales; a Tyler Perry commercial for his last stage play; and Judge Lynn Toler's Divorce Court. Michelle has starred or co-starred in eight stage plays, including *Where's My God Man* written by Evans Louissaint; *Damnation* written by Russell Tyson, *How to Love a Damaged Man* written by SistaGirl London and *True Love* written by Beverly Banks. Admiring such actors Denzel Washington, Regina King, Gabrielle Union and Tiffany Haddish, Michelle sees herself sharing scenes with them soon.

Today, Michelle is a radio host, author, actress, CEO of MemeAllOver and Life, Love & Lockup. In her spare time, she enjoys writing; studying acting; traveling; spending time with family and friends; researching natural products and information; and continuing her fight against Lupus. She resides in Atlanta, GA.

www.LifeLoveandLockup.com